American Empire

American Empire

A DEBATE

CHRISTOPHER LAYNE

BRADLEY A. THAYER

Routledge
Taylor & Francis Group
New York   London

Routledge is an imprint of the
Taylor & Francis Group, an informa business

Routledge
Taylor & Francis Group
270 Madison Avenue
New York, NY 10016

Routledge
Taylor & Francis Group
2 Park Square
Milton Park, Abingdon
Oxon OX14 4RN

© 2007 by Taylor & Francis Group, LLC
Routledge is an imprint of Taylor & Francis Group, an Informa business

Printed in the United States of America on acid-free paper
10 9 8 7 6 5 4 3 2 1

International Standard Book Number-10: 0-415-95204-2 (Softcover) 0-415-95203-4 (Hardcover)
International Standard Book Number-13: 978-0-415-95204-0 (Softcover) 978-0-415-95203-3 (Hardcover)

Library of Congress Cataloging-in-Publication Data

Layne, Christopher.
    American empire : a debate / Christopher Layne and Bradley A. Thayer.
      p. cm.
    Includes index.
    ISBN 0-415-95203-4 (hardback) -- ISBN 0-415-95204-2 (pbk.)
      1. United States--Foreign relations--2001- . 2. United States--Foreign relations--1989- . 3. Imperialism. 4. Hegemony --United States. 5. United States--Foreign relations--Philosophy. 6. United States--Military policy. 7. National security--United States. I. Thayer, Bradley A. II. Title.

E895.L39 2006
327.1--dc22
                                      2006016959

Visit the Taylor & Francis Web site at
http://www.taylorandfrancis.com

and the Routledge Web site at
http://www.routledge-ny.com

For my daughter and son, Ashleigh and Decebal, in the hope that they will live their lives in an America at peace and faithful to its ideals.

Christopher Layne

For the men and women of the United States armed services and intelligence community who have served their country in the past and today with great courage, patriotism, and professionalism. May Americans understand, acknowledge, and appreciate their sacrifice.

Bradley A. Thayer

Contents

Preface and Acknowledgments

This book is about America's post–Cold War grand strategy. We present two contrasting views. Bradley Thayer argues that the United States should maintain its current primacy in international politics and that America should use its military power, and the power of its culture and institutions, to advance and protect its interests. That includes a world order consistent with America's interests and its democratic ideology. In many respects, the strategy for which Thayer argues is, in fact, America's current grand strategy. In contrast, Christopher Layne argues that a grand strategy of primacy and empire is not in America's best interest. He argues that the strategy will lead to a geopolitical backlash against the United States, and that its aim of using American power to promote democracy abroad—especially in the Middle East—rests on dubious assumptions and will lead to unnecessary American military interventions abroad. Whereas Thayer believes the American Empire strengthens America's prosperity and security, Layne argues that the American Empire has high economic costs for the United States and weakens democracy at home.

This project grew out of the authors' friendship and shared interest in international relations theory and American foreign policy. Intellectually, we share much in common. We both were trained academically in the realist tradition of international relations theory. But as hundreds of hours of discussion over more than a decade of friendship have revealed, despite this commonality we have very different interpretations of realist theory and what realism implies for American grand strategy. The authors are tangible proof of the oft-cited dictum that realism is not a monolithic approach to the study of international politics. In addition to—or, perhaps more correctly, because of—our shared interest in international relations theory, we also have a strong interest in American grand strategy.

In academe, professors are expected to teach and to research. But—especially in a discipline like international politics that has profound real-world implications—we also have a duty to participate in public debates about U.S. foreign policy and to distill for nonacademics the theories and ideas that often drive U.S. behavior in the international system. At the end of the day, we are not only professors, but citizens. And as citizens we have a deep stake in ensuring that our nation remains secure and free. In this book, we hope to inform our readers and help them understand the pros and cons of two very different approaches to grand strategy that have the same goal.

We hope that after reading the two arguments presented here our readers will be better able to decide for themselves which of the two grand strategic visions presented here will best serve America's interests.

Grand strategy, what the military historian Edward Meade Earle called "the highest type of strategy," is the most crucial task of statecraft.[1] As historian Geoffrey Parker observes, grand strategy "encompasses the decisions of a state about its overall security—the threats it perceives, the way in which it confronts them, and the steps it takes to match ends and means...."[2] Distilled to its essence, grand strategy is about determining the state's vital interests—that is, those that are important enough for which to fight—and its role in the world. From that determination springs a state's ambitions, alliances, overseas military commitments, conception of its stakes in the prevailing international order, and the size and structure of its armed forces.

In formulating grand strategy, states must match their resources to their security requirements while simultaneously striking the proper balance between the competing demands of external and domestic policy.[3] Grand strategy requires the integration of the state's military and economic power, as well as diplomacy, to attain its interests. Thus, as Paul Kennedy observes, "The crux of grand strategy lies therefore in *policy*, that is, in the capacity of the nation's leaders to bring together all of the elements, both military and non-military, for the preservation and enhancement of the nation's long-term (that is, in wartime *and* peacetime) best interests."[4] Well-conceived grand strategies maximize the state's opportunity to further its interests peacefully. Flawed grand strategies can have a range of harmful effects, including overexpansion. In making grand strategy, therefore, it is important that policy-makers "get it right."

Grand strategy is not an abstract subject. 9/11 made this abundantly clear. Grand strategy is something that directly affects the lives and security—and even the prosperity—of all Americans. Events subsequent to 9/11 have confirmed this lesson. Along the Afghanistan/Pakistan border, U.S. troops continue to hunt for Osama bin Laden, and in Afghanistan itself, the United States—with support from NATO—is trying to suppress the remnants of the Taliban and establish a stable government. In Iraq, of course, the United States is involved in fighting an ongoing insurgency while simultaneously trying to prevent a civil war and assist the Iraqis in making a successful transition to democracy. Although there is no end in sight at this time to the American military involvement in Iraq, the United States finds itself involved in crises with both Iran and North Korea because of those two states' nuclear ambitions. And, of course—looming on the geopolitical horizon—China's rapid strides toward great power status raise important questions about the future of international politics generally, and about the Sino–American relationship specifically. All of these issues will affect Americans' lives in coming years and will be the subject of intense debate. We hope this book will contribute to that debate.

A word for our readers on how we wrote this book. Each of us wrote our main chapters (chapters 1 and 2) independently of the other. Only after these chapters were finished did we exchange them and read the other's argument. Our intent here was to avoid shoe-horning our arguments into a set template. Rather, we sought to allow each of us to make what he thought were the strongest arguments for his position. Our shorter reply chapters (chapters 3 and 4) were written after this exchange of chapters 1 and 2. Again, each of us wrote our reply chapters independently. Because this book constitutes a debate, it is the product of a collaborative exercise. However, because each of us wrote our contribution separately, those contributions are each single-authored works.

As with all intellectual projects, each of us has incurred debts to those who helped us. First, we both are grateful to Robert Tempio, who, while still at Routledge, encouraged us to undertake this project and nurtured it until he left to assume a new position with Princeton University Press. Second, we owe thanks as well to Charlotte Roh and Robert Sims of Routledge, who ably saw the book through at the end, and Kristin Crouch and Jennifer Gardner for their careful copyediting. Third, we are grateful to Professor Robert J. Art of Brandeis, who reviewed our book proposal for Routledge and strongly supported it. Fourth, but not least, we are deeply appreciative of the generous financial support we received from the Earhart Foundation, and we thank the Foundation's president, Ingrid Gregg, for her confidence in this project. Bradley Thayer thanks Nuray V. Ibryamova, Frank Russell, and C. Dale Walton for their outstanding comments. For their exceptional research assistance, Thayer is grateful to Caleb Bartley, Nicholas Gicinto, Austin McCubbin, Stephen B. Smith, Alaina Stephens, and Jason Wood. Christopher Layne thanks Gabriela Marin Thornton for her excellent comments. For her able research assistance, Layne thanks Sydney Woodington.

Notes

1. Edward Meade Earle, "Introduction," *Makers of Modern Strategy* (Princeton, N.J.: Princeton University Press, 1971), p. viii.
2. Geoffrey Parker, *The Grand Strategy of Philip II* (New Haven, Conn.: Yale University Press, 1998), p. 1.
3. Because they are expected to provide welfare as well as national security, modern states constantly face the dilemma of allocating scarce resources among the competing external and domestic policies. Arnold Wolfers, *Discord and Collaboration* (Baltimore: Johns Hopkins University Press, 1962). More generally, grand strategists must be cognizant of the danger that overinvesting in security in the short term can weaken the state in the long term by eroding the economic foundations of national power. This is the main theme in Robert Gilpin, *War and Change in World Politics* (Cambridge, UK: Cambridge University Press, 1981); Paul Kennedy, *The Rise and Fall of the Great Powers: Economic Change and Military Conflict from 1500 to 2000* (New York: Random House, 1987). This conundrum is a timeless aspect of grand strategy. As Edward Luttwak has observed, for both the Roman Empire and the United States, "the elusive goal of strategic statecraft was to provide security for the civilization without prejudicing the vitality of its economic base

and without compromising the stability of an evolving political order." Edward Luttwak, *The Grand Strategy of the Roman Empire: From the First Century A.D. to the Third* (Cambridge, Mass.: Harvard University Press, 1976) p. 1.

4. Paul Kennedy, ed., *Grand Strategies in War and Peace* (New Haven, Conn.: Yale University Press, 1991), p. 5.

1

The Case for the American Empire

BRADLEY A. THAYER

Countries and people are a lot alike. They have interests, objects that they love and want to protect against dangers and threats. They make choices about what they want to accomplish, and they strive to develop the means—ability, friends, or money—to help them reach their goals despite pitfalls and adversity. Just like people, countries come in all types. Some are rich and some are poor. Some are powerful and some are not. Some have great potential that has not yet been realized. They have a conception of their desires and interests, and how to advance them. This is the essence of grand strategy.

This book is about the grand strategy of the United States—the role Washington chooses to play in international politics. Some states have the freedom to vary their degree of involvement in the world, and the United States is one such state. It chooses to be the world leader, to maximize its interaction with the world; but it could choose to reduce its involvement and become isolationist if it so desired. Grand strategy is about these types of choices.

Grand strategy explains three things: the interests of states, the threats to those interests within international politics, and the means to advance interests while protecting against threats. The United States has interests, such as protecting the American people against threats, such as terrorists or nuclear war, and it has the means to do so because it procures a military: an air force, army, navy, and marine corps. It also has many allies who help it advance and protect its interests.

While all states have grand strategies, they differ in their means to advance their interests in the face of threats. France has greater means than Bangladesh. The United States has the greatest means. In fact, the United States finds itself in a special position in international politics: by almost any measure—economic, ideological, military—it leads the world. It is the dominant state, the hegemon, in international politics. If you stop and think a moment, it is really remarkable that 6 percent of the world's population and 6 percent of its land mass has the world's most formidable military capabilities, creates about 25 to 30 percent of the gross world product, and both attracts and provides the most foreign direct investment of any country. If it were a person, it would have the wealth of Microsoft chairman Bill Gates or entrepreneur Donald Trump; its

1

military would have the punch of a heavyweight boxer like Muhammad Ali or Mike Tyson; its charisma and charm would equal those of a movie star such as Cary Grant or George Clooney; and it would have as many friends, hangers on, and potential suitors as Frank Sinatra did at one time or as Oprah or Britney Spears do now.

This book is a debate about the rightful place of the United States in the world. What are America's interests in the world? How should it use its power to advance those interests? Is America's preeminent place in international politics a force for good in the world? I argue that it is.

Thinking about America's grand strategy is important for two major reasons. First, It affects all Americans and, indeed, people the world over from Afghanistan to Zimbabwe. In sum, you may not be interested in America's grand strategy, but America's grand strategy may be interested in you. If you are an American, it influences you by determining whether you fight in a war, how you fight it, and with whom. It affects America's economy, and that makes it easier for you to find employment or to keep you from employment. So it is important for Americans to think about the role their country plays in the world and whether they believe it to be the right one. People in other countries are also influenced by how America acts, the countries it sees as allies and enemies, as well as by what countries and resources it chooses to defend. The American people derive much benefit from America's predominant place in the world but it also entails significant costs. While I believe that the benefits outweigh the costs, at the end of the day it is for the American people as a whole to decide if that is so.

Second, understanding grand strategy—and specifically primacy—permits a more sophisticated consideration of why America acts in world politics, as it does, what it values, and what it will defend. When you grasp America's grand strategy, you are able to predict how the United States will behave in the future and answer many questions, including why the United States acts essentially the same way in international politics in Democratic and Republican administrations. While there are differences, both Democrats and Republicans want a strong American military, economic, and political presence in the world. Both are willing to use force to defend America's interests. The Clinton administration intervened in Bosnia and Kosovo, as the Bush administration did in Iraq. You can also see why the United States has military and intelligence bases in more countries now than when we faced the threat from the Soviet Union during the Cold War, and why the United States wants to keep those bases. Understanding the American grand strategy of primacy grants you the ability to perceive what America's vital interests are and the threats to those interests and to predict how the United States will act against threats to maintain its key interests.

Because it is such an important subject that touches on what America's interests ought to be, Americans disagree about grand strategy. There are three major schools of thought: isolationism, selective engagement, and primacy. Proponents of isolationism argue that the United States should withdraw from involvement in international politics and devote more resources to domestic social problems.[1] Selective engagement submits that the United States should only possess sufficient strength to defend the centers of economic might in the world, principally Europe and northeast Asia.[2] Advocates of primacy assent that the United States should be the major power in international politics and must keep its preponderant position in international politics by maintaining its military and economic strength.[3]

My argument fits into the primacy school of thought. I advance my argument in three sections. First, I examine the motivation and spirit of the American Empire from its inception. I submit that its origins date to the founding of the country. The desire to spread the influence of the United States filled the spirits of the Founding Fathers. Second, I address the question: *Can* America remain dominant in the world? I argue that it can for the foreseeable future. Third, I consider the critical issue: *Should* America strive to retain its prominent place in global politics? I submit it should indeed do so because it is the right action for the United States at this point in its history.

The Spirit of the American Empire: More the Expansion of Ideas and Influence than of Territory

Is America an empire? Yes, it is. An empire is a state that surpasses all others in capabilities and sense of mission.[4] An empire usually exceeds others in capabilities such as the size of its territory and material resources. Its capabilities are much greater than the average or norm prevailing in the international system.

Second, an empire has worldwide interests. Its interests are coterminous with boundaries of the system itself, and the interests are defended directly by the imperial states or by client states. That is, there is literally almost nothing that does not concern the United States; from Paraguay to Nepal, or Sweden to New Zealand, the United States has interests there it seeks to protect. As the comedian Jeff Foxworthy would put: "You know you are an empire when...." You know you are an empire when other states cannot ignore you and must acquiesce to your interests, but you do not have to satisfy theirs. Other states, willingly or not, define their positions, roles, or actions in relation to the imperial power, rather than to their neighbors or other states. Diplomats in New Delhi first worry about "What will Washington think?" rather than "What will Islamabad, or Kabul, or Harare, think?"

Third, empires always have a mission they seek to accomplish—this is usually creating, and then maintaining, a world order. The details of the world order broadly match the interests of the imperial state. For Rome, it was obedience to the Senate and people of Rome. For France, it was Catholicism, French political control, and French language and culture. For the United States, it has been a free economic order, democracy, and human rights.

While almost the entire world agrees that the United States is an empire, it is not according to American leaders. They almost never use the "E word." It is as if they had never heard the word "empire." They prefer to speak of American "leadership," or "direction," "the key role of the United States" in the Western "community" or "civilization."

Of course, it is not surprising that American leaders suffer a memory lapse when it comes to the word empire. They choose not to use it because it does not help to achieve the grand strategic goals of the United States. To do so would make their lives more difficult because it would aid resistance to the American Empire. For an American president or senior official to state that America is an empire would only help to organize resistance to it. To say it is an empire might cause the American people to question whether or not they want one. To say it plainly would only help those who do not wish the American Empire well.

After all, there is a reason a used car salesman calls a used car a "pre-owned" one. Both buyer and seller know the car is used. But using the euphemism "pre-owned" helps both. For the seller, it helps to focus the buyer's attention away from some of the unpleasant consequences of owning a "used" car, and the buyer benefits because he thinks he is getting something better than a "used" vehicle.

Accordingly, American leaders are right not to call attention to the American Empire, as this would only increase balancing forces against it, and thus would ultimately be damaging to its continuation. Also, not mentioning the word helps to ensure that U.S. political leaders are careful not to be gratuitously arrogant or boastful. The leaders of the United States seem to be following the advice of French statesmen in the wake of the Franco–Prussian War. The French defeat caused it to lose important territory—the provinces of Alsace and Lorraine—to Germany. The French claimed that it was the duty of French statesmen and citizens to "think of them always, but speak of them never." So it is with the American Empire. American leaders and the American foreign policy community must labor mightily to ensure the expansion and maintenance of the American Empire, but they should never tout or gratuitously boast of it: "think of it always, but speak of it never."

While American leaders may not use the "E word," plenty of others do—from all around the world. In fact, in 1998, French foreign minister Hubert Védrine found that "superpower" was too weak a word to describe the power of the United States, so he created a word, "hyperpower," to describe its formidable capabilities. The French are not the only ones to notice. The Chinese leadership's warnings of the risks of one country becoming too powerful are as constant and rhythmic as a drumbeat. Not to be left behind, worldwide media such as the BBC and *al Jazeera* television lament the unpleasantness of living in a world dominated by Uncle Sam's Empire.

America Is a Unique Empire

The answer to the question is yes, America is an empire, but it is a unique empire. When we consider the subject, we realize that each empire is different in scope, in size, and in its place in history, but the United States is the most singular of all empires. It certainly is not an empire in the traditional sense of a country that occupies others. It is true that America has gained a lot of territory. The United States has expanded greatly since its founding in 1776, and it has occupied other countries, but most of its territory it acquired peaceably from the French (1803), Mexicans (1853), Russians (1867), or Hawaiians (1898), and its territorial expansion stopped at around 1900. In fact, after becoming a strong country, America's desire and need to occupy territory was less than when it was weaker, in the eighteenth and nineteenth centuries. While it has occupied countries, such as Japan and parts of Germany, after World War II, its occupations were short—certainly if you compare the American Empire to all others, including the British and Roman, which occupied lands for hundreds of years.

Then, in what sense is America an empire? What unites any empire is control over weaker states or, before there were states, other political units like tribes. That was true of all the great empires in the past—Athens, Alexander the Great's Macedonia, Byzantium, Carthage, China, Rome, France, Great Britain, Mongol, Ottoman, Portugal, Russia, Spain—and it is true of the United States now. Other empires sought direct control over other political units (states or city-states like Athens or Carthage), and, once gained, maintained and spread their control. Think of Rome controlling through occupation the known world or Spain occupying almost all of the New World after 1492.

As Table 1.1 indicates, the United States is like those empires because, fundamentally, every empire is concerned with control—it wants its goals realized and its interests preserved. But in most respects—and these are more important than the similarities — the United States is not like those empires. Table 1.1 explains the important differences with respect to the type of rule, the need for territorial and ideological expansion, the openness of its economic system, the degree to which the imperial state uses its own military forces to conduct wars or fight with allied states, and the amount of interaction between its military—for training and education—and other militaries. This last point is particularly important because few Americans realize that their military is a "mini–State Department." It conducts its own diplomacy with the militaries of other countries and works to train and educate them, as well as to learn from them, to benefit the foreign and American militaries. The preferred instrument of the United States is to control indirectly, through countries that share its ideology and want to align their country with

Table 1.1 A Comparison of Traditional Empires with the American Empire

	Traditional Empires	**American Empire**
Main objective	Control	Control
Type of rule	Direct	Indirect
Expansion of territory	Very important	Less important
Expansion of ideology	Of little importance for the Imperial State	Very important
Openness of the Imperial Economy	Closed to outsiders	Open to all
The use of the Imperial Military and its degree of interaction with other militaries	Use of own forces to conduct wars Little interaction with other militaries	Own military forces often used with allies to conduct wars Much interaction with other militaries

the United States. Now, keep in mind that the United States is no shrinking violet of a country. It will not shy from using its "hard power"—its military or economic might—when it must. Examples of hard power include imposing economic sanctions on countries or attacking them. The United States is certainly willing to use hard power. It has invaded Panama, liberated Kuwait, intervened in Bosnia, fought a war with Serbia over Kosovo, and invaded Iraq since the end of the Cold War. But it prefers to use "soft power," because soft power is the most effective way of influencing countries over a long period of time. Think of soft power as getting others to do what you want through the attractiveness of the political ideas of the United States and its culture.[5] If countries share the same goals and have the same expectations about international politics, then cooperation between them will be easier.

The American Empire differs from other empires because, most often, the United States is concerned with influencing the foreign policies of other states, principally leaving their domestic policies alone. For example, Washington sets the tone for most of the 26 countries of the NATO alliance, as well as Australia, Japan, the Philippines, South Korea, Taiwan, and Thailand. There are differences, to be sure, and at times these can be quite vociferous; for example, consider the strong French objections to the invasion of Iraq. But most of the time the foreign policies of these states dovetail with the United State's political goals. Because of the strains in America's relations with France and Germany caused by the Iraq war, Americans often forget that the French, Germans, and other NATO allies have soldiers in Afghanistan who fight alongside Afghani and American soldiers.

The United States seeks to maintain control not through occupation of territory but through other means, such as expanding its ideology of democracy and free market economics; it freely permits access to its economy by other countries. And it will, if necessary, threaten the use of military force to protect and advance its interests, and if required, it will use force for those ends. Occasionally, it will act explicitly like other empires and occupy other countries. Recently, it has occupied Afghanistan and Iraq. In the past, it has occupied many countries, including the Dominican Republic, Haiti, Nicaragua, and the Philippines.

But the United States is a unique empire. It is very different from all of those that have come before. The American Empire stands in marked contrast even to the British Empire, with whom it shares an ideology and economic system. It is not interested in the expansion of territorial control by conquering territory and imposing colonial rule. It is interested in promoting the political and economic well-being of its allies. Of course, the American Empire stands in even greater contrast to the world's other empires, most of which were principally interested in exploiting their colonies as efficiently and rapidly as possible.

In September 1943, in a speech given at Harvard University, Winston Churchill made a remarkable comment about the future of imperial power: "The empires of the future," he said, "are the empires of the mind." That is the American Empire. It does not covet territory or resources. It covets ideas. The American Empire is an empire of ideas, and its ideas are those that led to its founding in 1776. These ideas are the "Spirit of 1776."

The Spirit of 1776

If the United States is an empire, why is it one? After all, the United States could retreat into isolationism. Instead, it chooses to be an empire. In order to comprehend why, you have to understand the political motivation or political spirit of the American Revolution of 1776.

I argue that when you understand the spirit of the American Revolution, you understand why the United States is an empire. The expansion of the United States was what the Founding Fathers wanted for their country—the expansion of its territory and its ideas. But like most critically important topics, people can disagree over this. Americans should disagree about what America's interests are, not in 1776, but today.

In essence, the heart of the debate in this book is whether this vision, the spirit that animates the American Empire, is the right one for the United States today. I strongly believe it is. Christopher Layne, equally strongly, believes it is not. People—and Americans in particular—should think through the central issue considered in this book and make their own judgments about the value and costs of the American Empire.

The political spirit of the American Empire predates 1776, before the United States was even a country. In fact, the spirit of the American Empire helped to create the American Revolution. The desire to spread the creed or ideology of America has animated the politics and political figures in the

United States from the earliest days. Consider the impassioned speeches of Patrick Henry and Thomas Jefferson or the writings of James Madison, Thomas Paine, and George Washington. "However unimportant America may be considered at present," Washington wrote to the Marquis de LaFayette in 1786, "and however Britain may affect to despise her trade, there will assuredly come a day, when this country will have some weight in the scale of Empires."[6] Throughout his presidency, Jefferson declared that the United States was "an empire for liberty" and described it as "a chosen country" and a "rising nation" that was already "advancing rapidly to destinies beyond the reach of the mortal eye."[7] In 1809, he wrote to James Madison that it was the genius of the American government that would permit "such an empire for liberty as she has never surveyed since the creation; and I am persuaded no constitution was ever before so well calculated as ours for extensive empire and self-government."[8]

If you really want to understand the American Revolution—the motivation of the Founding Fathers—you also have to turn to the writings of Thomas Paine. As he did so often, Paine summarized the political spirit of the American Revolution: "From a small spark, kindled in America, a flame has arisen, not to be extinguished. Without consuming...it winds its progress from nation to nation, and conquers by a silent operation," and when men know their rights they are free, and despotism is destroyed because "the strength and powers of despotism consist wholly in the fear of resisting it."[9]

For America's Founding Fathers, Paine's view was common. In addition, they believed that the United States had a responsibility to spread its values and institutions in a world dominated by antiliberal forces, principally monarchy and its guiding principle, the Divine Right of Kings—the belief that God had chosen certain people to rule over others in His name. For the Founding Fathers, the world was in great need of the enlightenment provided by republican government. They would not have questioned either the superiority of American ideals or the flow of the tide of history in the direction of their universal application. And very few would have questioned the legitimacy of spreading America's values around the globe. That was the mission of the United States of America.

The spread of the flame of the American ideology through Paine's "silent operation" has often been effective, but relying on it has never been sufficient to destroy those deemed despots by American leaders. The United States, like many other empires, has depended on hard power and soft power to realize the expansion of its influence.

This spirit of the American Revolution meant that the United States has wanted to expand its influence since before its birth in 1776—and actually even before its birth it tried to do so. The expansion of its influence came in two forms. First was its territorial expansion, and the United States satisfied its appetite by 1900. The second was its expansion through the influence of its ideology.

Although it is as old as the desire for territorial expansion, the prodigious appetite of the United States for ideological expansion has never been satisfied.

Few Americans recall how hungry for territory their country was in the eighteenth and nineteenth centuries. Indeed, even before it had declared its independence—while it was still in the womb—it coveted Canada and attempted to seize it. In 1775, Congressional President John Hancock ordered General Philip Schuyler to conquer Montreal.[10] This failed, as did many subsequent attempts. The rapidity of the expansion of the United States from thirteen colonies in 1776 to the status of a hegemon some two hundred years later is startling.[11] It really is remarkable, and too few Americans reflect on it.

Think about this point for a minute. In about a person's lifespan the United States came to dominate the North American continent. The country more than doubled its size with the Louisiana Purchase of 1803 not even thirty years after its founding. By 1819, it had added Florida to its territory. About seventy years after its creation, it had gained the independent Republic of Texas and all of the West. Or perhaps more accurately, reacquired Texas, since some historians think it was included in the Louisiana Purchase, but John Quincy Adams gave much of it away when he negotiated the United States border with Spain. When the United States was about ninety years old, it almost doubled its size with the purchase of Alaska from Russia. A large part of the explanation for this expansion lies with the recognition that the United States has long had the dream of empire, and now that has been fulfilled.[12]

Its expansion and rise to its present status in international politics was made possible by a desire to expand and share its values in the world. John Quincy Adams captured this force well when, in 1819, as secretary of state to President James Monroe, he wrote that it was the "proper dominion" of the United States to possess all of North America including what is now Mexico and Canada, from "the time when we became an independent people it was as much a law of nature that this should become our pretension as that the Mississippi should flow to the sea."[13] Of course, the desire to expand was not solely the passion of Yankees but was shared below the Mason–Dixon Line. The Confederate States of America had aspirations to conquer the Caribbean and much of Latin America once the war was over, and I wonder if the Confederate States of America would have realized their ambition had positions been reversed at Appomattox in 1865.

The rise of the United States to hegemonic status would not surprise many of the Founding Fathers or other observers such as the preeminent economist Adam Smith and the great political commentator Alexis de Tocqueville. In 1776, Smith wrote "From shopkeepers, tradesmen, and attornies [sic]," the American colonists have become "statesmen and legislators, and are employed in contriving a new form of government for an extensive empire, which, they flatter themselves, will become, and which, indeed, seems very likely to become, one of the greatest and most formidable that ever was in the world."[14] In 1846,

Tocqueville wrote of the United States and Russia that they "have grown in obscurity, and while the world's attention was occupied elsewhere, they have suddenly taken their place among the leading nations, making the world take note of their birth and of their greatness almost at the same instant." And while Tocqueville admitted significant differences between the two countries, he saw presciently that "each seems called by some secret design of Providence one day to hold in its hands the destinies of half the world."[15]

Tocqueville's vision would be realized, but it took time for America's capabilities to match its ambitions. And it took a Civil War. The United States endured great vulnerability and dangerous adversity in its early years, including the Civil War, which ensured that the United States could become a great power. It could do so because it would remain united and thus more powerful than two United States—north and south—who would struggle against each other and be used by European great powers to advance their own ends in North and South America. The second reason the Civil War was important for the rise of the United States was that it confirmed the power of a federal government that could harness and organize the great resources of the country efficiently—infinitely better than fifty state governments attempting to do the same thing.

Of course, the political spirit of the Revolution did not completely account for the speed of American expansion. One general point deserves to be made. And that is that, frankly, in its history, the United States has been (and remains) an extremely lucky country. Its geography is lucky. It was far enough away from Europe to make the projection of military power to North American difficult, as British King George III found out to his chagrin. The Atlantic and Pacific Oceans are formidable moats that America's enemies have found very difficult to cross.

In addition to its geographical good luck, two other elements were present. The United States was blessed with weak neighbors, such as Mexico, which were not able to prevent its expansion. Second, only European great powers possessed the ability to arrest American expansion, but they did not because of the threat of war in Europe or the distractions of maintaining their empires.

Sometimes European powers even supported American expansion. Britain backed Jefferson's Louisiana Purchase in order to ensure that French power was removed from the North American continent. Expansion by the weak United States was acceptable to London, but France was a formidable military power. French territory in North America was a threat to British interests. It could have become a base to reconquer the great expanse of North America that it lost to Britain at the conclusion of the Seven Years' War in 1763. However, most frequently, the United States expanded while countries such as France and Great Britain were occupied with European concerns.

Nevertheless, we should not underestimate the fear—rightly held by America's early presidents—that European powers would block the expansion of the

United States to the west, or even use their territory in North America to move against the United States when events in Europe were stable enough to allow them to act. Britain was the biggest concern and, occasionally, the United States acted to preempt British territorial conquest. Today, few Americans realize that Monterey—the premier California port at the time—was seized by the U.S. Navy in 1842, four years before the start of Mexican–American War, due to reports that a strong British force had sailed from Chile and that war had started between the United States and Mexico, and that Britain would seize the port first and occupy California in the name of protecting Mexico. After a short occupation, Monterey was returned to Mexican authorities. Of course, the U.S. Navy would be back in four years—this time to stay.

In the meantime, the United States initiated what today we would call a covert action campaign to encourage the residents of California to rebel against Mexico and declare their independence. Here the United States was following the precedent it set in Texas a decade earlier. In fact, U.S. agents distributed copies of the Texas Constitution to encourage Californians to declare independence, at which time the United States could intervene. To advance this objective, explorer John Frémont and his fifty well-armed men not only scouted Mexican territory, as the history books record, but also attempted to encourage rebellion, combat British influence, and contact American agents in the territory. However, these actions did not have much success before Congress declared war on Mexico in 1846.

So, when we reflect on the history of America's foreign relations and the motives of the Founding Fathers and those statesmen who followed in their path, we realize that it is a false dilemma to believe that the history of American foreign relations was wholly internationalist or absolutely isolationist. As the eminent historian Felix Gilbert wrote of the Founders' foreign policy ideas: "American foreign policy was idealistic and internationalist no less than isolationist" and often existed side by side.[16] Those who look for absolute consistency in the foreign policy ideas of the Founding Fathers are bound to be disappointed. Some were isolationists. Some were expansionists. Most, however, were realists par excellence, swinging from isolationism to internationalism with ease, with no concern for consistency, only, for the interests of the United States.

However, the great majority of the Founding Fathers, if not all, saw the United States as a special country, whose founding and ideals were like no other, and whose mission was to share its ideology with other peoples. To discover the spirit that animated them, simply look at the Great Seal of the United States on the back of the dollar bill. The mottos on the seal of the United States are *Annuit coeptis* (God has blessed this undertaking) and *Novus Ordo Seculorum* (A New Order for the Ages), and these truly capture the spirit of America's founding and mission. The Founding Fathers did believe that they had created a special country, an empire of liberty, whose benefits should be shared by the rest of the world and, in turn, whose existence threatened despotic regimes and was threatened by them.

Can America Dominate the World? Yes, Through Hard and Soft Power

The United States has the ability to dominate the world because it has prodigious military capability, economic might, and soft power. The United States dominates the world today, but will it be able to do so in the future? The answer is yes, for the foreseeable future—the next thirty to forty years.[17] Indeed, it may exist for much longer. I would not be surprised to see American dominance last much longer and, indeed, anticipate that it will. But there is simply too much uncertainty about events far in the future to make reliable predictions.

In this section of the chapter, I explain why the United States has the ability to dominate the world for the predictable future, if it has the will to do so. There are two critical questions that serve as the foundation for this debate: "Can America dominate international politics?" and "Should America dominate international politics?"

The U.S. military, economy, and soft power answer the first question—these elements give it the ability to do so. How long the American Empire lasts depends on three variables: first, its hard and soft power capabilities; second, the actions of other states; and third, its will to continue its empire. America's ideology answers the second issue. These critical questions are inextricably linked. The United States has the ability to dominate the world, but that is only one of the key ingredients necessary for the "meal of empire." The will to do so is equally important. If the United States does not have the will, then no amount of combat aircraft or ships or economic might will suffice to ensure its dominance in international politics. I will consider the second issue in the next section of this chapter.

At the outset of this discussion, I want to state an obvious but, nonetheless, salient point: Nothing lasts forever. The American Empire will end at some point in time, as every empire has in the past—from the empire the Egyptian Pharaohs created over 2,800 years before Christ to the one forged by Lenin's Bolsheviks in 1917—and as future empires will as well. As Table 1.2 shows, the American Empire is young when compared to the other empires throughout history, having lasted just over a century if we take the beginning of the Spanish–American War as its starting date, as conventional history often does. Although it may be young, it is the profound responsibility of the custodians of the American Empire to use hard and soft power to ensure that it lasts as long as they want.

Hard Power—American Military Supremacy

The U.S. military is the best in the world and it has been so since end of World War II. No country has deployed its forces in so many countries and varied climates—from the Arctic to the Antarctic—from below the sea to outer space.

Table 1.2 The Longevity of Selected Empires throughout History

Empire	Duration	Longevity (Years)
Egypt	2850–525 B.C.	2,325
Byzantine	A.D. 330–1453	1,123
Rome	509 B.C.–A.D. 476	985
Venice	A.D. 1000–1799	799
Assyria	1363–612 B.C.	751
Portugal	A.D. 1420–1999	579
Ottoman	A.D. 1350–1918	568
Caliphate (Abassid)	A.D. 750–1258	508
France	A.D. 1515–1962	447
China	206 B.C.–A.D. 220	426
Britain	A.D. 1585–1997	412
Spain	A.D. 1492–1898	406
Netherlands	A.D. 1602–1949	347
Seleucid	311–63 B.C.	248
Persia	559–330 B.C.	229
Russia	A.D. 1700–1917	217
Sweden	A.D. 1561–1718	157
America	A.D. 1898–Present	108+
Mongol	A.D. 1206–1294	88
Athens	478–404 B.C.	74
Soviet Union	A.D. 1917–1991	74
Italy	A.D. 1882–1947	65
Germany	A.D. 1871–1918	47

No country is better able to fight wars of any type, from guerrilla conflicts to major campaigns on the scale of World War II. No country or likely alliance has the ability to defeat the U.S. military on the battlefield. Thus, measured on either an absolute or relative (that is, comparing the U.S. military to the militaries of other countries) scale, American military power is overwhelming. Indeed, it is the greatest that it has ever been.

This is not by accident. The United States has worked assiduously, particularly since 1940, to produce the best military. The causes of American military predominance include extensive training and professional education, high morale, good military doctrine, frequency of use, learning from other militaries in the right circumstances, exceptional equipment and sound maintenance, and high levels of defense spending.

The United States spends roughly $420 billion a year on defense.[18] This amount does not include spending on nuclear energy–related activities, such as insuring the viability of the nuclear weapons stockpile ($17.5 billion more in fiscal year 2006), or other defense related activities, such as military help for the FBI or Secret Service (add $3.2 billion more). It also does not include defense spending "supplementals," which cover the expenses incurred in Afghanistan and Iraq (about $82 billion). Astonishingly, that is about half of total world defense spending.

No other country, or group of countries, comes close to matching the defense spending of the United States. Table 1.3 provides a context for this defense spending through a comparison of the defense spending of major countries in 2004, according the International Institute for Strategic Studies (IISS). The United States is far ahead of the defense spending of all other countries, including its nearest competitor, China. This is by design. As former Speaker of the House of Representatives Newt Gingrich has argued, "You do not need today's defense budget to defend the United States. You need today's defense budget to lead the world. If you are prepared to give up leading the world, you can have a much smaller defense budget."[19] To maintain the robust American lead in military capabilities, it must continue to spend large, but absolutely affordable, sums.

And it is affordable. While the amount of U.S. defense spending certainly is a large sum, it is only about 4 percent of its gross domestic product, as Table 1.3 illustrates. An examination of the data in the table is remarkable for four reasons. First, U.S. defense spending is about half of the world's total defense spending. Second, the United States spends more than almost all the other major military powers in the world combined. Of course, most of those major military powers are also allies of the United States. Third, U.S. defense spending is very low when measured as a percentage of its economy, about 3.7 percent of its total economy. Fourth, defense spending at that level is easily affordable for the United States into the future.

In fact, in absolute real terms, the United States spends about 10 percent more on defense than it did during the Cold War. If we examine the history of defense spending during the Cold War, only in fiscal years 1946, 1951–1953, 1967–1969, 1983–1990 did the United States spend more on defense when measured in fiscal year 2005 dollars.[20] And because the U.S. economy was smaller, the defense spending burden was greater in those years; it is much less now. Nor is the burden of military service too great for the American people to bear. As Table 1.3 demonstrates, there are only about 1.5 million people in uniform, out of a population of 300 million, or approximately 0.5 percent of the population. In comparison, during World War II, when the U.S. population numbered some 140 million, about 13 million people, or nearly 9 percent of the population, were in uniform.

Table 1.3 A Comparison of the Top 25 Countries' Defense Expenditures, per Capita Expenditures, Percentage of GDP, and Armed Forces in 2004

Rank/Country	US$M (% of World Total)	Defense Expenditure in US$ per Capita	Defense Expenditure as % GDP	Numbers in Armed Forces (Thousands)	Estimated Reservists (Thousands)
1/United States	455,000 (46)	1,552	3.8	1,473.9	1,290.9
2/China	62,500 (6)	47.8	3.7	2,255	800
3/Russia	61,900 (6)	431	4.4	1037	2,000
4/France	51,600(5)	850	2.6	254.8	21.6
5/Japan	42,442 (4)	333	0.9	239.9	44.4
6/United Kingdom	49,600 (5)	821	2.3	205.9	272.5
7/Germany	37,700 (3.8)	457	1.4	284.5	358.6
8/Italy	30,500 (3)	524.9	1.83	191.9	56.5
9/Saudi Arabia	19,300 (2)	775	8.1	199.5	NA
10/India	19,600 (2)	18	3.0	1,325.0	1,155
11/South Korea	15,488 (1.6)	318	2.3	687.7	4,500
12/Australia	14,300 (1)	711.78	2.4	52.8	20.8
13/Turkey	10,100 (1)	145	3.4	514.8	378.7
14/Israel	9,680 (<1)	1,542	8.2	168.3	408
15/Canada	11,400 (1)	350	1.1	62	36.9
16/Spain	12,500 (<1)	309.8	1.2	147.2	319
17/Brazil	9,230 (<1)	49.6	1.6	302.9	1,340
18/Netherlands	9,600 (<1)	585	1.6	53.1	54.4
19/Greece	5,860 (<1)	549.2	2.9	163.8	325
20/Taiwan	7,211 (<1)	314	2.37	290.0	1,657
21/Indonesia	7,550 (<1)	31.2	3	302	400
22/Myanmar (Burma)	6,230 (<1)	126.2	9	428	NA
23/Sweden	5,439 (<1)	605	1.59	27.6	262
24/Ukraine	6,000 (<1)	125.7	1.9	187.6	1,000
25/North Korea	5,500 (<1)	240	2.5	1,106	4,700
World total	997,158 (100)				

Notes: All data for 2004. NA = Not Available.

Source: Data from International Institute of Strategic Studies, *The Military Balance 2005–2006*, (London: Oxford University Press, 2005) passim. Data from Stockholm International Peace Research Institute (SIPRI), *SIPRI Military Expenditure Database* available at: <http://www.sipri.org/contents/milap/milex/mex_database1.html>.

Another critical question is not simply how much the United States spends on defense but what benefits it receives from its spending: "Is the money spent worth it?" The benefits of American military power are considerable, and I will elaborate on five of them. First, and most importantly, the American people are protected from invasion and attack. The horrific attacks of 9/11 are—mercifully—an aberration. The men and women of the U.S. military and intelligence community do an outstanding job deterring aggression against the United States.

Second, American interests abroad are protected. U.S. military power allows Washington to defeat its enemies overseas. For example, the United States has made the decision to attack terrorists far from America's shores, and not to wait while they use bases in other countries to plan and train for attacks against the United States itself. Its military power also gives Washington the power to protect its interests abroad by deterring attacks against America's interests or coercing potential or actual opponents. In international politics, coercion means dissuading an opponent from actions America does not want it to do or to do something that it wants done. For example, the United States wanted Libya to give up the weapons of mass destruction capabilities it possessed or was developing. As Deputy Defense Secretary Paul Wolfowitz said, "I think the reason Mu'ammar Qadhafi agreed to give up his weapons of mass destruction was because he saw what happened to Saddam Hussein."[21]

Third, our allies like Australia, Great Britain, Japan, Kuwait, Israel, and Thailand are protected by American military might and so we are able to deter attacks against them. They are aligned with the United States, and thus under its "security umbrella"—any attack on those states would be met by the military power of the United States. Other states know this and, usually, that is sufficient to deter aggression against the allies of the United States.

Fourth, as political scientist Barry Posen has argued, military power gives the United States control over the global "commons," the command of the sea, air, and space, that allows it effectively to project its power far from its borders while denying those areas to other countries if it so chooses.[22] That is significant because the sea lanes, airspace, and space act as a major force multiplier for the United States, allowing Washington to exploit better its own economic and military resources and those of its allies while at the same time hindering its enemies. For example, control of the world's oceans provides the United States with the ability to move heavy forces to trouble spots such as the Persian Gulf or Korea and ensure that key resources, like oil, may travel to world markets. Command of space gives the United States control of the ultimate "high ground." The United States owns about half of the approximately three hundred active satellites in the Earth's orbit. Its intelligence satellites allow it to spy on the rest of the world; its navigation satellites guide its forces; and its communications satellites give Washington the ability to command forces worldwide.

Fifth, the military power of the United States gives it great influence in international politics. This influence comes in several forms, one of which is the U.S.' ability to create favorable conditions in international politics, such as by securing access to key regions of the world like the Persian Gulf. Often the United States does this by creating global partnerships for action. As a general rule, these partnerships are easy to create because most states want to cooperate with the United States, leading to broad partnerships with like-minded states to advance common interests.

A second key form of influence occurs through military training and the other military-to-military contacts conducted by the Pentagon. Although most Americans do not know this, the U.S. military and State Department train a large number of foreign military officers, about sixty thousand a year, through its worldwide educational programs, such as the International Military Education and Training (IMET) program. They conduct joint exercises on a bilateral or multilateral basis worldwide, and run a program to aid militaries in operating and maintaining U.S. equipment. Officers and civilian officials from 158 countries in Africa, Asia, Europe, Latin America, and the Middle East participate and are taught many aspects of military operations—from military leadership to the latest combat lessons learned from Iraq, to dealing with the media and avoiding human rights abuses. This benefits the officers because they learn from the world's best military—it is like a premier baseball team, such as the New York Yankees, giving tips to minor-league teams. Those teams would want to learn from the stellar ball clubs so that they may improve their game and benefit from the experience of others. Additionally, foreign civilian leaders want to expose promising military officers to the training to inculcate the officers with a proper conception of the role of the military in democratic states and respect for civilian control.

Of course, such military-to-military cooperation also benefits the United States. First, it helps the United States convey its values to the students, many of whom will become senior military leaders in their countries. Students through firsthand experience better understand American life, ideals, and democratic politics. For example, students are taught to respect civilian control of the military and not to abuse enemy prisoners or civilians. Students are also introduced to the U.S. Constitution and Bill of Rights; they are informed how local, state, and federal governments operate in the United States; and they are educated on many other topics related to American politics and culture.

Additionally, it provides the United States with influence on a personal and professional level. Foreign military officers may make friends with their American military instructors and that may lead to a solid and warm working relationship between individuals as they rise in military rank and influence. Professionally, it makes cooperation between the American and foreign militaries easier because it fosters greater appreciation of U.S. interests and the interests of other U.S. allies. Students also improve their English language skills, a very practical step toward making communication easier. Moreover, foreign militaries know how the U.S. military is organized, functions, trains, and how it conducts operations. They understand as well that the U.S. military is second to none and so is the right choice to emulate. In turn, this increases the likelihood that the U.S. military will serve as a template for foreign militaries as they reform and become more professional; secondly, a grasp of how the U.S. military operates increases the chances that intermilitary cooperation will be more effective and harmonious since all parties involved will be calling plays from the same playbook.

While there might be concern that foreign militaries are learning all of the secrets of the U.S. military, there is, in fact, little danger that foreign military education will hurt the United States. Its high level of military effectiveness is not only the product of the classroom; it stems from the synergy created by motivation, doctrine, training, force structure, equipment, and experience.

In January 2005, Deputy Defense Secretary Wolfowitz summed up the value of the exchange programs when he toured Indonesia in the wake of the tsunami cataclysm of December 2004. He said that "we've mitigated some of the problems" in the cooperation between the United States and Indonesian militaries coordinating the disaster relief "by the fact that many Indonesian officers, including the current President of Indonesia," who was democratically elected, "have been to the United States, have been trained in the United States, understand what it means to have civilian control over the military, and have relationships with our officers."[23] The bottom line for such cooperation, he continued, is that "those kinds of relationships also make it possible to respond much more quickly and effectively in a crisis like this one."[24] Such cooperation saved countless lives after the 2004 tsunami.

Although the United States is the dominant military power at this time, and will remain so into the foreseeable future, this does not mean that it does not suffer from problems within its own military, many of which are being addressed. The "defense transformation" efforts started by Secretary of Defense Donald Rumsfeld are attempts to make the U.S. military more combat effective and efficient. The U.S. military is the best, but no one would claim that it is perfect. However, a large part of the reason the U.S. military is the best is because it is constantly evaluating its problems so that it may solve them. Many people do not realize this. Despite a common image of the military in American popular culture as lowbrow and full of Cletus-the-Slack-Jawed-Yokel characters from *The Simpsons* television show, the military is comprised of some of the smartest and best-educated people you will ever meet. Most mid- and high-ranking officers have master's or even doctoral (Ph.D.) degrees. These are people who would be very successful in corporate careers but choose the military because of their patriotism and desire to serve their country.

Nevertheless, the military prowess of the United States does not mean that states or terrorist groups will not attack it. Perfect deterrence of all attacks is not possible—the United States may still be attacked at home or abroad and will always be vulnerable to some type of attack. The military and intelligence community are, and must always remain, vigilant because, although they succeed in protecting Americans the vast majority of the time, they are judged by failures like Pearl Harbor or 9/11. Moreover, although it is rare, history shows that weaker states do attack stronger ones, as Japan did in 1941, or as Egypt and Syria did when they attacked Israel in 1973. But if a country were foolish enough to attack the United States, it is very likely to be defeated soundly and absolutely defeated and this fact helps maintain the massive deterrent power of the United States.

Of course, being so powerful does not mean that the United States always gets what it wants. Like people, countries have free will, including the ability not to follow the American lead. The invasion of Iraq in 2003 is a case in point. Much has been made of the decision of major NATO allies like France and Germany not to participate in the Iraq war. Diplomatically, of course, it would have been better for the United States had they done so.

Nonetheless, in its fifty-year history, the NATO alliance has faced crises and survived them. Indeed, it survived many worse ones in far more difficult strategic conditions during the Cold War, when the profound threat from the Soviet Union existed. There were serious fights over German rearmament, a shared European nuclear force called the Multilateral Nuclear Force, French President Charles de Gaulle's withdrawal from NATO's military mission, and the deployment of modern, intermediate-range nuclear forces in the early 1980s.[25] It is certain that NATO will face crises in the future. In fact, crises for NATO are like subway trains—you may expect that they will come along at regular intervals—and if you miss one, don't worry, there will be another one soon.

The military contribution of the French and Germans was not necessary to the Iraq invasion, and their absence underscored the power of the U.S. military. However, our NATO allies do support us in Afghanistan. Those who criticize the Bush administration for being "unilateral" seldom recognize that, while France and Germany chose not to participate in the Iraq war, all NATO countries, including France and Germany, have been greatly supportive of Operation Enduring Freedom in Afghanistan. In fact, the French started flying combat missions in Afghanistan on October 21, 2001. French forces have been there ever since—including French special forces. At the time of this writing, the French have about 1,500 troops supporting combat operations in that country. That is about 10 percent of all forces. So, in reality, our allies are supporting the United States in major combat operations, just not in Iraq. Their soldiers face the risks of combat alongside American soldiers—fighting side by side just as they did in World War II.

When the totality of the evidence about the American military is examined, there has never been a country with such preponderant military might. In both absolute and relative terms, and barring some tremendous folly, America will continue to dominate the world's other militaries for the foreseeable future.

Hard Power—American Economic Might

American economic power is critical to the maintenance of the American Empire because economic power is the wellspring of military power. A good rule of thumb in international politics is that a country's gross domestic product equals the strength of military power, or GDP = Military Power. So, a healthy American economy helps to ensure adequate military strength to preserve America's position in the world. Fortunately for the United States, it has the world's largest economy and its relative economic strength, like its relative military power, is astonishing.

In order to demonstrate this argument, we have to examine the aggregate economic strength of the United States versus the economic power of other countries. Table 1.4 captures the relative economic might of the United States. It provides a comparison of the world's top twenty economies as estimated by the Central Intelligence Agency, the International Institute for Strategic Studies, and the World Bank. For the United States, the data are consistent using any of the major tools economists employ to estimate economic might (the CIA's GDP-PPP, GDP for the IISS, and GNI for the World Bank). The data show that the United States is clearly the world's most powerful economy in both absolute and relative terms.

Indeed, if we consider economies, only the twenty-five-member-nation European Union (EU) possibly surpasses American economic might, and if it does, it is not by much. In 2004, the EU's economy was $11.05 trillion, in contrast to the $10.99 trillion U.S. economy in 2003, according to the CIA.[26] If we recognize that the CIA estimates the EU had 1 percent real growth in 2004, and the United States had 3.1 percent real growth in 2003, it is the case that the economies are really the same size. Additionally, as I will describe below, the U.S. economy is much more efficient and better primed for continued economic growth than is the EU's sclerotic and moribund economy.

The United States is the world's largest and most efficient economy. Its currency is the world's reserve currency, it fosters and protects international trade and helps to serve as the "lender of last resort" for the world economy. Additionally, the United States is enjoying historically low levels of inflation, unemployment, and interest rates. However, despite this unrivaled economic dominance, no economy is perfect. The U.S. economy certainly has problems, such as a large federal budget deficit and a considerable current account deficit (the difference between what Americans earn from and pay to foreigners).

Continuing deficits have made the United States the world's leading debtor. But neither deficits nor debt are a major problem for the United States.

The federal budget deficit may be serviced by selling bonds, raising taxes, or reducing the spending of the federal government. Unlike the budget deficit, the current account deficit is not something the United States wholly controls since it involves international trade. The United States must borrow money from abroad to service the debt if Americans choose not to save their disposable income. And Americans love to spend, rather than save, their money.

Much of the current account deficit is due to China and, to a lesser extent, Japan. That actually is good news for the current account deficit of the United States because the Chinese, Japanese, and other central banks in East Asia have an enormous stake in selling to the United States. These economies depend on exports, and the United States is an enormous market for their products and services. To ensure that their currency is weak against the American dollar, which is good for their export industries, they keep buying dollars and securities based on the dollar.

If they did not, the dollar would lose value against the Chinese currency (the renminbi), causing Chinese imports to cost more, resulting in fewer Americans buying them, in turn causing a loss of jobs and downturn in the Chinese economy at a critical time—millions of Chinese are moving from rural areas to the cities to seek manufacturing jobs. If there were a substantial downturn in the Chinese economy, unemployment could lead to political unrest. The communist leaders of China are acutely aware of this, since economic problems fueled the revolution in which they took power.

Prominent historian Niall Ferguson estimates that if the dollar fell by one-third against the renminbi, the Chinese could suffer a loss of about 10 percent of their GDP.[27] That would be catastrophic, and so it is unacceptable to the Chinese. Thus, China's economic interest requires it to fund the current account deficit of the United States. "The United States may be discovering what the British found in their imperial heyday," Ferguson writes; that is, "If you are a truly powerful empire, you can borrow a lot of money at surprisingly reasonable rates. Today's deficits are in fact dwarfed in relative terms by the amount the British borrowed to finance their Global War on (French) Terror between 1793 to 1815"—and the British Empire lasted another 150 years.[28]

Despite problems, the American economy is both huge and robust, and it continues to grow at healthy rates. Depending on how one counts the numbers, the U.S. economy accounts for between 20 to 30 percent of world GDP. Moreover, the United States is the world's most productive country and still leads the world in innovation according to the World Economic Forum (WEF), an organization that measures the competitiveness of countries around the world.

Each year, it publishes a ranking of each country's economic competitiveness. This is comprised of the quality of the macroeconomic environment of a given country, the health of its public institutions, and its technological

Table 1.4 A Comparison of the Top 20 Countries' Economic Strength from the CIA, IISS, and World Bank

Rank/Country (Rank by CIA 2004 GDP data)	CIA (2004)			IISS (2004)			World Bank (2003)			
	GDP ($ billions)	per Capita ($ thou.)	Population (millions)	GDP ($ billions)	per Capita ($ thou.)	Population (millions)	GNI ($ billions)	per Capita ($ thou.)	Population (millions)	Rank (by 2003 GNI data)
1/United States	10,990	37,800	293	11,700	40,047	293	11,012	37,870	291	1
2/Japan	28,200	3,582	127	4,660	36,598	127	4,360	34,180	128	2
3/Germany	2,271	27,600	82	2,670	32,472	82	2,085	25,270	83	3
4/United Kingdom	1,666	27,700	60	2,130	35,488	60	1,680	28,320	59	4
5/France	1,661	27,600	60	2,000	33,201	60	1,521	24,730	60	5
6/Italy	1,550	26,700	58	1,660	28,685	58	1,243	21,570	58	7
7/China	6,449	5,000	1,298	1,680	1,293	1,306	1,416	1,100	1,288	6
8/Russia	1,282	8,900	143	1,400	9,779	143	374	2,610	143	16
9/Canada	958.7	29,800	32	980	30,146	32	773	24,470	32	8
10/Spain	885.5	22,000	40	986	24,488	40	700	17,040	41	9

11/Mexico	941.2	9,000	104	664	6,335	106	637	6,230	102	10
12/South Korea	857.8	17,800	48	673	13,973	48	576	12,030	48	11
13/India	3,033	2,900	1,065	648	609	1,080	570	570	1,064	12
14/Brazil	1,375	7,600	184	581	3,160	186	479	2,720	177	13
15/Netherlands	461.4	28,600	16	575	35,255	16	425	26,230	16	15
16/Australia	571.4	29,000	19	598	30,059	20	436	21,950	20	14
17/Switzerland	239.3	32,700	7	361	48,450	7	299	40,680	7	17
18/Belgium	299.1	29,100	10	349	33,762	10	267	25,760	10	18
19/Sweden	238.3	26,800	9	340	37,923	9	258	28,910	9	19
20/Austria	245.3	30,000	8	290	35,487	8	216	26,810	8	20

Notes: For CIA data, GDP dollar estimates for all countries are derived from purchasing power parity (PPP) calculations rather than from conversions at official currency exchange rates. The PPP method involves the use of standardized international dollar price weights, which are applied to the quantities of final goods and services produced in a given economy. The data derived from the PPP method provide the best available starting point for comparisons of economic strength and well-being between countries. For World Bank data, GNI (formerly referred to as gross national product, or GNP) measures the total domestic and foreign value added claimed by residents. GNI comprises GDP plus net receipts of primary income (compensation of employees and property income) from nonresident sources.

Source: From CIA, CIA World Factbook, online edition available at: http://www.cia.gov/cia/publications/factbook/. Data from IISS, *The Military Balance 2005–2006*, (London: Oxford University Press, 2005). Data from World Bank, *2005 World Development Indicators*, (Washington, D.C.: The World Bank, 2005).

sophistication. Traditionally the United States is ranked first or second. In 2004, it was ranked second of 104 countries, behind only Finland (China is 46th). According to the World Economic Forum, the United States "is ranked second, with overall technological supremacy, and especially high scores for such indicators as companies' spending on R&D [research and development], the creativity of the scientific community, personal computer and internet penetration rates."[29] Also in 2004, the United States was first in the WEF's rankings for business competitiveness (China is 47th) and technological innovation (China is 104th) a critical indication of long-term prosperity. Nor is the 2004 ranking an aberration; the United States historically ranks first in those categories of global competitiveness.

The U.S. economy continues to grow and, most importantly, much of its productivity is based on the information technology (IT) revolution. Significantly, this is not the case in Europe or Japan, where substantial growth has yet to occur (as in Europe) or has peaked (as in Japan). According to economist Deepak Lal, the "big difference in the productivity increases between the U.S. and Europe has been in the sectors that are substantial *users* of IT equipment and software," and these industries are the key to continued economic growth in the information age.[30] The United States's lead in IT may be overcome at some point, perhaps by China, but not in the foreseeable future, as the United States remains the world's IT leader. In turn, this helps to ensure the military dominance of the United States, as so much military technology depends on information technology.

Given the historical economic growth rates of these countries, it is unlikely that any of them (or the EU) will be able to reach the levels of economic growth required to match current U.S. defense spending and, thus, supplant the United States. China comes closest with 6.6 percent annual economic growth estimated by the World Bank through 2020, or the 7 percent annual economic growth estimated by the World Economic Forum through 2020.[31] It is not even clear if China can sustain its growth rates and, other than China, no other country is even in the ballpark. Table 1.5 shows the sustained economic growth rates necessary to match the present military spending by the United States.

Thus, the economy is well placed to be the engine of the American Empire. Even the leading proponent of the "imperial overstretch" argument, Yale University historian Paul Kennedy, has acknowledged this. Imperial overstretch occurs when an empire's military power and alliance commitments are too burdensome for its economy. In the 1980s, there was much concern among academics that the United States was in danger of this as its economy strained to fund its military operations and alliance commitments abroad. However, Kennedy now acknowledges that he was wrong when he made that argument in his famous book, *The Rise and Fall of the Great Powers*, because of the robustness of American economic and military power. Indeed, if there is any

Table 1.5 Economic Growth Rates (%) Required to Match Present U.S. Military Spending (as % of GDP)

	2020	2050	2100	Actual GDP Growth Rate 1973 to 1998
China	8.5	5.2	4.1	6.84
France	14.3	7.4	5.2	2.10
U.K.	14.6	7.5	5.2	2.00
India	11.8	6.4	4.7	5.07
Russia	12.7	6.8	4.9	−1.15
EU	6.5	4.4	3.7	NA

Note: Assumptions: US$ real PPP GDP will grow at a constant 3 percent per year (averaged from 1988 to 1998). $ Military expenditures/GDP will stay the same as in 2000.

Source: From Lal, D., *In Praise of Empires: Globalization and Order*, (New York: Palgrave Macmillan, 2004), p. 72. With permission.

imperial overstretch, it is more likely to be by China, France, Britain, India, Russia, or the EU—not the United States.

Reflecting on the history of world politics, Kennedy submits that the United States not only has overwhelming dominance but possesses such power so as to be a historically unique condition: "Nothing has ever existed like this disparity of power; nothing. I have returned to all of the comparative defense spending and military personnel statistics over the past 500 years that I compiled in *The Rise and Fall of the Great Powers*, and no other nation comes close," not even an empire as great as the British, because "even the Royal Navy was equal only to the next two navies. Right now all the other navies in the world combined could not dent American maritime supremacy."[32] Moreover, Kennedy recognizes that the steady economic growth of the American economy, and the curbing of inflation, means that "America's enormous defense expenditures could be pursued at a far lower relative cost to the country than the military spending of Ronald Reagan's years," and that fact is "an incomparable source of the U.S. strength."[33]

When Kennedy, who was perhaps the strongest skeptic of the economic foundation of America's power, comes to acknowledge, first, that no previous empire has been as powerful as America is now; and, second, that its strength will last because of the fundamental soundness of its economy, then, as Jeff Foxworthy would say, "You might be an empire...." And it is one that will last a considerable amount of time. As with its military might, the economic foundation of the American empire is sound for the projected future.

Soft Power—The Power of Ideas

The soft power of the United States is considerable. We are able to persuade many countries to work with us, whether in military actions like Iraq, or in the economic realm, such as in the World Trade Organization. Why do other countries often want to work with the United States? This is so for two major reasons.

The first reason is self-interest. Countries may help the United States because they want to seek favor from Washington. For example, by participating in the occupation of Iraq, a country like El Salvador earns good will in Washington. At some point in time, El Salvador will remind U.S. officials of that when it needs a favor from Washington. This is what political experts call "logrolling," or, put another way, "If you scratch my back, I'll scratch yours."

The second reason is soft power. Other countries want to work with the United States because they share its goals and want what the United States wants. This is not logrolling. They help because they really want to, not with the expectation that they will receive some specific reward. At some point, the soft power of the United States has changed their opinion, so that individuals or countries that once opposed the United States now understand its actions, and, most often, support them. The soft power of the United States goes far in explaining why the United States has so many allies and so much support in other countries.

How do you get somebody to want what you want—how does soft power work? Soft power works through formal (governmental) and informal (nongovernmental) means, and I will discuss each in turn. The United States spreads its soft power through governmental agencies like the National Endowment for Democracy, which has helped budding democracies, such as the Ukraine, by aiding the citizens of new democracies to learn how to participate in open, fair, and free elections. The United States spreads its ideals and furthers its goals through the Fulbright scholar programs sponsored by the Department of State. One Fulbright program—the Fulbright Foreign Language Teaching Assistance Program—brings graduate students from abroad to U.S. campuses to teach native languages that are in high demand in the war on terror, but where there are few American speakers and teachers. These languages include Arabic, Urdu, and Uzbek.

The alumni of the Fulbright programs certainly are distinguished: they have won 34 Nobel prizes and 65 Pulitzer prizes; 21 have received MacArthur Foundation "genius" awards, and 14 have been awarded presidential Medals of Freedom, the highest honor the United States can bestow on a civilian. More than that, Fulbright alumni have risen to the height of power in many countries and helped to advance American interests and principles. These include Armindo Maia, who helped lead East Timor's struggle for freedom and democracy, and a Fulbright scholar at Stanford, Alejandro Toledo, who was once a shoeshine boy and is now president of Peru.

Other formal vehicles of soft power include *Radio Sawa*, radio programming that attempts to influence people in the Middle East. With a budget of only $22 million, it heavily emphasizes popular music, with news reports mixed into the programming. It has largely displaced *Voice of America* as the major U.S. government–sponsored radio outlet for the Middle East and has been particularly effective in attracting Arabs in the 15- to 30-year-old demographic range. In fact, April 2004 surveys conducted by the polling company A.C. Nielsen found the network to be the most successful one in the Middle East. Like *Radio Sawa*, the *Al Hurra* television station is backed by the U.S. government, with the same objective and audience.

These media outlets are important, but are only one vehicle for soft power. The State Department spends about $340 million a year to support democracy in the Middle East through the Middle East Partnership Initiative, the National Endowment for Democracy, and educational and cultural exchanges.

In January 2003, to further the soft power capabilities of the United States, the White House created the Office of Global Communications to coordinate strategic communication with global audiences and provide advice concerning how to reach foreign audiences. Shortly before, National Security Advisor Condoleezza Rice established a Strategic Communication Policy Coordinating Committee that would work with all federal agencies to harmonize the President's message to the rest of the world. No doubt, there is a problem for the United States—and the Pentagon's Defense Science Board concluded that the U.S. strategic communication effort suffers from four problems: (1) a lack of presidential direction; (2) insufficient interagency coordination on what America's message to the world ought to be; (3) the government and the private sector (such as Hollywood) are not yet full partners in strategic communication; and, (4) inadequate resources to support America's message.[34]

Although Internet penetration of the Middle East is low, it is growing rapidly. The United States must expand its interactive, content-rich, web-based broadcasting. Arab and Muslim Internet users are more likely to be the opinion makers whom the United States will want to influence. Web sites sponsored by the United States or allied governments are an important mechanism to influence opinion.

Annual spending on State Department information programs and U.S. international broadcasting such as the *Voice of America* and *Radio Marti* broadcasting to Cuba is approximately $1.2 billion, or about one-quarter of one percent of the military budget, and about equal to what McDonald's spends on advertising. The disconnect between a military budget four hundred times greater than a strategic communication budget is unacceptable when the global war on terrorism is largely about ideas and perceptions of the United States. That should change. Soft power takes time, but it is about establishing relationships with key players worldwide, journalists, educators, film and theater actors and directors, and business leaders.

Informal soft power mechanisms are even more important than government programs. Nongovernmental groups and organizations are an enormous help to the U.S. government, and many private organizations work to build democracy as well. One of the most important of these is the Carter Center, founded by former President and First Lady Jimmy and Rosalynn Carter. The Carter Center fosters democracy abroad by monitoring elections, promoting the rule of law, and developing the ability of civic organizations to participate in government policy making.

Education is also a great informal source of soft power. The United States' higher educational system is perhaps the most important vehicle for transmitting American values. Former Secretary of State Colin Powell captured its significance well when he stated "I can think of no more valuable asset to our country than the friendship of future world leaders who have been educated here."[35] Admitting foreign students to study at American colleges and universities has a long history in the United States. During the Cold War it was particularly important, with over fifty thousand Soviet academics, writers, journalists, and artists visiting from 1958 to 1988. There is no doubt that Soviet espionage agents were sent to the United States to spy, but it also the case that the program served to undermine the Soviet Union. A former participant was KGB agent Oleg Kalugin, who became one of the highest ranking defectors to the West. Kalugin said that U.S.–Soviet exchange programs were a Trojan horse for the Soviet Union that played a tremendous role in the erosion of the Soviet system, as they "infected" more and more people with Western ideas over the years.[36]

Education is also big business. Educating foreign students is a $13 billion industry for the United States with critical implications for American industry. This is because many graduate students in engineering and the natural sciences come to the United States to study but gain employment and stay in the country, often becoming citizens.

As a consequence of its premier educational institutions and leadership in graduate education, there is an incredible concentration of intellectual ability in the United States. There are some six hundred thousand foreign students studying in the United States annually. Most of the best universities and private and public think tanks are in the United States, and most of the greatest scientists and top scholars conduct their research in the United States.

Although native English speakers may not think of it, the English language itself is a great ally of the American Empire. The English language is the world's lingua franca. It is spoken as a native language by about 400 million people, an almost equal number know it fluently as a second language, and many more know some words and phrases precisely because it is indispensable for business, diplomacy, the Internet, higher education, navigation, and travel. It is reported that more than 300 million Chinese—the equivalent of the population of the United States—are studying English.

The spread of English facilitates communication and mutual influence, allowing people the world over to participate in the same colloquium, thanks to which Russian and Brazilian academics can exchange ideas and pass them along to Japanese intellectuals. A businessman in Istanbul is able to sell to someone in Beijing. There are tens of millions of people who conduct business in English and yet have never had a transaction with a native English speaker. It is even the official language of the European Central Bank. For two years, the Pew Research Center for People and the Press polled sixty-six thousand people from forty-four countries concerning whether children "need to learn English to succeed in the world today." More than 95 percent of those surveyed in Indonesia, Germany, and South Africa agreed, as did more than 90 percent of those surveyed in China, Japan, France, and the Ukraine.[37]

But by far the most influential soft power vehicle for the United States is its film and television industries. Most of the world watches American films and television. It is an enormous market. The film industry alone makes about $100 billion a year, and about half of its revenue is earned from overseas markets; that amount was just 30 percent of revenues in 1980. Indeed, what it estimates it loses to the piracy of movies, $3 billion, is the total revenue of some industries and is the equivalent of the gross domestic product of some countries. Indeed, it is about three times the GDP of Burkina Faso. The success of America's entertainment industry is due in no small measure to the storytelling skills of its actors, directors, and producers.[38]

It can be hard to realize how films and television influence people. After all, people usually watch a film or television for entertainment, not to be influenced. But, in fact, these are some of the most effective media for advancing ideas, because people lose themselves when they watch entertainment. Their guard drops and they are then more easily influenced than if they were being lectured to by a professor, their parents, or a politician. They want to be in the movie theater or watch the television because it is fun. A film, or other "cultural goods," such as theater, books, or television, conveys ideas, symbols, and ways of life, entertaining and shaping the ideas of the audience at the same time. They establish collective identity and common experience (we have all seen the films *Titanic* and *The Godfather*) and influence what people say, what they think, how they act, how they dress, and how they talk to others.

A second reason is that film and television have a particularly great influence on young people. In many countries around the world, young people watch a lot of films and television; starting at an early age and for much of their lives, they will be influenced by American ideas. Moreover, young people are easier to influence than older people because they have less experience and want to learn how to fit in—what they should say, how they should act, and what they should think. Grandma already knows how to act, but the grandchildren do not; her opinions are forged by a lifetime of hard experience—that is not true for her grandchildren, who have little experience and thus are easier to shape.

Film and television tell people what they should say in a particular situation, how they should think, and how they should live their lives. The ideas may be advanced through the dialogue, by how the characters act, or, even more subtly, such as in the background. If you are from New York City and you travel abroad, people will think you live like the characters on *Friends*; if from California, everyone will think you live like the characters on *Beverly Hills 90210*; and if you are from Texas, the show *Dallas* got there before you did to influence people's image of Texas, or California, or New York City. Television has shaped their conception of you. They saw it, after all, and if we see it, then we often think it is true. This is the key reason why Hollywood and television stars complain about typecasting or getting fans to recognize that they are not the characters they play—if Christopher Walken or James Woods always play creepy characters, then they must be creepy; if Nicole Kidman is inevitably the "good girl" in her roles, then she must be good. People often see screen or television actors and think of them as friends or enemies, good or bad, although they have never met them and never will.

We have this problem because we trust our senses—they have been good to us over the course of human evolution. But the 4 to 5 million years of human evolution did not equip us for Steven Spielberg's films or American television. They have a formidable power precisely because we trust our senses. A typical person in Pakistan may think that everyone in California lives on the beach, drives fancy cars, and dates everyone who comes through the door. And they want to live that way too. Of course, the reality is that some Californians do live that way, but the vast majority do not. Certainly, not all elements may be attractive to people in Pakistan or Indonesia or Kenya, but enough of it is to be effective because it appeals to humans universally. The image is more important than reality and it shapes opinion—what people think about the United States, our freedoms, and the lives of people in this country.

Of course, people watch entertainment not to be influenced by political ideas; the ideas piggyback on the entertainment. You watch because you are entertained, and you keep watching because you are captured by the story. Therefore, you are more likely to be influenced by messages subtly presented rather than by a blunt, explicit work such as the great Soviet director Serge Eisenstein's *Battleship Potemkin*. And American filmmakers are very good at keeping people watching. As Philip Adams, the former head of the Australian Film Commission has said: "A country that makes a film like *Star Wars* deserves to rule the world."[39]

Key to the success of the American Empire is that people want many of its products, and that desire provides the United States with considerable soft power. Although he was certainly no fan of American power and culture,

Arthur Koestler, the author of *Darkness at Noon*, saw that the key to U.S. power was that people wanted what America provided. In 1951, he recognized that the growth of American influence in Europe was mainly due to the Europeans themselves: "The United States does not rule Europe as the British ruled India; they waged no Opium War to force their revolting 'Coke' down our throats. Europe bought the whole package because Europe wanted it."[40]

Koestler saw a fundamental truth. America delivers what many people want because it appeals to human universals—whether it is rock 'n' roll, consumption captured by the trope "shop till you drop," or important liberties, like free speech. People welcome American ideas and culture as being not "from above," imposed by government, but rather as being "from below"—people want and seek American cultural products even in the face of resistance from their government, as is the case today in Iran. Soft power spreads American ideas and popular culture from below, and the potency of America's ideas and popular culture should never be underestimated.[41]

America's soft power, its ideas, culture, and language, are as important as the military and economic foundations of America's Empire. Like those, there is no sign that America's soft power is waning—just the reverse: its ideas, culture, and language are more popular than ever before. In fact, given the popularity and strength of Hollywood and American television in the world, it may be expected to grow in attractiveness to the world's population.

Are American Capabilities Able to Address the Threats the United States Now Confronts: China, the European Union, and Islamic Fundamentalist Terrorism?

The United States does not exist in a vacuum. What other states and terrorists do is centrally important for how long the United States is able to maintain its dominant position. In this section of the chapter, I will consider three issues: the threat from China, the potential threat of the European Union, and the danger presented by Islamic fundamentalist terrorism. China and the European Union are important to consider because they have the potential economic power to supplant the United States as the global hegemon.

Will they be able to supplant the United States? Probably not, but it is hard to tell over the course of the twenty-first century—after all, Yogi Berra once said that predictions are hard, especially about the future. Despite the difficulties of prediction, two types of dangers affect the projected paths of any country. First, and by definition, unforeseen events cannot be predicted but, of course, could occur—think of a revolution that forever changed a country's path, like those in China in 1949, Iran in 1979, or Russia in 1917. The second, foreseen problems, may be identified because the seeds of danger have been planted already. I will focus on these. Both China and the European Union face major problems hindering their economic growth and thus their ability to challenge the United States for preeminence in international politics. I will address the problems confronting each in turn. Then I will address the problem of Islamic fundamentalist terrorism.

The Threat from China: Significant, but Reduced by the Dragon's Demographics China is a major country undergoing a dramatic modernization process. It is where the United States was a hundred years ago or where most major European countries were one hundred and fifty years ago. Periods of modernization result in great economic growth as economies move from agrarian to an industrial or postindustrial information economy. Its economic growth rates are very impressive—an 8 percent real increase in GDP in 2000, 7.3 percent in 2001, 8 percent in 2002, and 9.1 percent in 2003.[42] So the trend of economic growth is clear and certainly will continue for the next few years, before falling off as economic efficiencies and returns on trade decline. Eventually, China will have economic growth rates of 1 percent, 2 percent, or 3 percent per year, which is typical for developed countries.   Nevertheless, as a result of its rapid growth, China will be in a position to threaten the dominant role of the United States in world politics. According to the National Intelligence Council, China is projected to have about a $4.3 trillion GDP in 2016.[43] That is equivalent to the 2003 GDP of Japan. About 2042, China is expected to have the GDP (about $10.9 trillion) that the United States possessed in 2003.

Although its continued economic growth is impressive, China faces major problems that will hinder its ability to replace the United States as the world's hegemon. The first of these is a rapidly aging population beginning in 2020. Nearly 400 million Chinese will be over sixty-five years old by 2020. This could be a source of unrest and economic stagnation. Younger generations will be pressed to care for the older population. There will be a great discrepancy between the numbers of young people and the elderly, and China lacks the pension and health care infrastructure characteristic of Western societies. Many Chinese will have to work far into old age and will not be able to care for themselves should they fall sick or be too old to earn a wage. As we see with Japan, economic productivity will peak.

This situation is the direct result of the "one child" policy adopted in 1979 to halt explosive population growth. When China took its first countrywide census in 1953, its population was 600 million. By 1970, it was approximately 800 million. As a result of the "one child" policy, the Chinese birthrate has fallen from 5.8 children per woman in 1970 to fewer than 2 per woman in 2000. The "one child" policy is believed to have resulted in 300 million fewer Chinese.

A second big problem stemming from the "one child" policy is the imbalance between the sexes. For social and economic reasons, if only one child is permitted, most Chinese parents will choose a son. This has led to widespread abortion, female infanticide, and female adoption out of China. Simply put, there are too few females in China. The normal worldwide divergence between the number of boys to girls is about 103 males to 107 females. In China, about

119 boys are born for every 100 girls. In rural areas, where the preference for sons is the strongest, the imbalance is even greater, about 133 to 100.[44] There are an estimated 40 million more men than women in China's population.

The declining birth rates that flow from this will hinder economic growth in the long run. China eventually will face other major economic and social problems as well, including those related to the economic fragility of its financial system and state-owned enterprises, economic malaise brought on by widespread corruption, ubiquitous environmental pollution, HIV/AIDS and other epidemic diseases like SARS, and the high energy costs, which stifle economic growth. In addition, unlike the United States, China is not a model for other countries. Chinese political values are inferior to those of the United States because China is repressive. The Chinese do not respect human rights, including religious and political freedom.

There is also the wildcard of potential conflict over Taiwan. A war with Taiwan would retard China's economic progress and scare neighboring states. The fact that China has so many territorial and other disputes with its major neighbors, Japan, India, Russia, and Vietnam, means that many countries see it as a threat and will want to ally with the United States against Chinese power. The rise of China is ripe for potential conflict with its neighbors, and this constitutes a big danger in international politics.

The Threat from the European Union: Lessened by Demographics and Decadence   The European Union is the second alternative to the dominance of the United States. The European Union has 25 members and is likely to add Bulgaria and Romania by 2007; Croatia by 2009; and Macedonia, and, perhaps, Turkey shortly thereafter. EU states have almost 500 million people and an economy slightly larger than the economy of the United States. Additionally, most EU members use a single currency, the euro, which is replacing the dollar as an international reserve currency. The United States, in turn, is forced to pay higher interest rates to central banks and other investors around the world to induce them to buy U.S. Treasury bonds. This is by design, as Romano Prodi revealed when he was the European Commission's president: "The euro is just an antipasto....It is the first course, but there will be others. The historical significance of the euro is to construct a bipolar economy in the world. The unipolar world is over. There are two poles now: the dollar, and the euro."[45] No doubt, Prodi and other EU officials would like to see American economic dominance supplanted by European hegemony. Indeed, it is safe to assume that their ambitions are not limited to economic dominance.

In addition to its economic might, the EU has a modest defense force, the European Rapid Reaction Force (ERRF), of about sixty thousand soldiers, sailors, and airmen. The ERRF is wholly independent of NATO and is beginning to act as a coherent force. In 2003, it undertook a peacekeeping mission to Macedonia, Operation Amber Fox, replacing a NATO operation there. This was the first allied military mission in Europe since the end of World War II that did not include U.S. forces. In 2004, the EU launched another mission, Operation Althea (also known as EuFor), in Bosnia. The EUFOR mission of seven thousand troops is designed to take over most of NATO's responsibilities (for what NATO called SFOR, or Stabilization Force), which includes maintaining stability and enforcing the 1995 Dayton Agreement.

Yet unlike China, the EU simply does not pose a great danger to the American Empire for two major reasons—political and socioeconomic. The political similarities between the EU and the United States are enormous. In essence, the political values of EU are largely those of the United States. This is not a surprise, in many respects; the United States is the daughter of Europe, and that may be excellent news for future warm relations between them. In addition, if the "clash of civilizations" argument made famous by Samuel Huntington is correct (that is, that future major conflicts will be between civilizations), then as other civilizations become more powerful—such as the Chinese or Islamic—Europe and the United States will be united again by the threat from those civilizations.[46] They were united during the Cold War by the threat from the Soviet Union, and history teaches that an external threat can produce comity where once there was rivalry.

In addition to the political reasons, there are three major socioeconomic reasons why the EU will not be able to challenge the United States. These are (1) the costs of expansion; (2) the different approach to work and the related costs of generous social welfare programs in the EU; and (3) the aging EU workforce and the risks of Muslim immigration to the EU's identity.

The first factor retarding economic growth is the costs involved in the further expansion of the European Union. Expansion is hindered by the fact that Brussels has only a fraction of the structural funds (aid to regions or countries where GDP per capita is below 75 percent EU average, such as Portugal, Greece, Spain, and the former East Germany) needed to bring new members up to the standard of living found in the rest of the EU. Additionally, new members will receive no cohesion funds, which are given to build a country's infrastructure. The simple fact is that there is too little money for too many new members (already about 35 percent of the EU budget goes to the structural and cohesion funds).

This situation stands in stark contrast to the 1970s and early 1980s when Ireland, Portugal, Spain, and Greece joined. At that time, the number of rich members and the small number of new members meant that the funds were well focused. That is not true today. As a result, the EU will be tiered: wealthier old members will continue to receive generous structural and cohesion funds, while new members occupy a second, poorer tier.

The Common Agricultural Policy also hinders economic growth in the European Union. Almost half (about 45 percent) of the EU's budget is spent on agriculture—mostly payments to farmers. The EU provides about $120 billion in agricultural subsidies. In contrast, the U.S. government provides about $40 billion annually in agricultural subsidies. Each cow in the United States gets about $120 a year in federal subsidies. Each European cow gets $600 per year from the EU.[47] These subsidies are an enormous drain on the EU economy but are perpetuated because EU members do not want to lose them.

The second economic reason is that EU is based on a different socioeconomic model than the United States. The American economy is as close as it gets to raw capitalism. You have to work to feed, house, and clothe yourself in America. The social safety net does have large gaps in comparison to Europe, and there is great disparity in wealth—a smaller number of people have control over more of the wealth of the country than in Europe. America is a great place to be rich. It is in Europe as well, but less so due to high taxes and greater income equality. The ratio between what the top tier of American CEOs earn and what the average manufacturing employee earns is 475:1. In Europe, the ratio is 24:1 in Britain, 15:1 in France, and 13:1 in Sweden. On the other hand, the American economy is fluid, so the guy who invents the better mousetrap is able to market it and make a million. There is relatively little government intervention in the economy, and capitalism is warmly embraced. America is the epitome of free market capitalism.

The European economy does not work that way. In contrast to America, there is much more government intervention in the economy—laws that govern business practices and protect workers and the environment—and there is great ambivalence toward capitalism. Europeans prefer a closer distribution of wealth so that there is not an enormous gap between the richest and the poorest. In the United States, about 20 percent of adults are living in poverty, while the numbers are about 7.5 percent for France, 7.6 percent for Germany, 6.5 percent for Italy, and 14.6 percent for Britain. Europeans strongly prefer a social safety net. A system of cradle-to-grave welfare programs exists to help Europeans receive an education and to shelter people from the storms of life, even if they are tempests that affect health, housing, or employment. European unemployment rates are consistently higher than those in the United States because the costs of being unemployed are much lower due to the social safety net than in the United States, where modest unemployment benefits soon are exhausted.

Americans also work much harder than Europeans. In 2003, Americans worked an average of 1,976 hours. German and French workers averaged about 400 fewer hours per year. One American in three works more than 50 hours a week. It is the rare European who matches those hours. Vacations are generous for Europeans, about 5 weeks, as are holidays. Employees have 23 paid holidays in Britain, 25 in France, and Sweden has 30. In the United States, depending in which state you reside, you get 4 to 10 holidays.[48] In sum, Americans work much harder than Europeans.

But social welfare is expensive. It requires high taxes to support generous government spending. This, in turn, hinders economic growth. So, too, does maintaining tight income equality. If you tell someone that he will be able to earn only a certain amount, and no more than that, he does not have an incentive to work hard (although he does have an incentive to move to America, where he can become rich). Slow economic growth and high unemployment is known as "Eurosclerosis," and the disease shows no signs of being cured anytime soon. The lack of economic growth results in a lack of funds for research and development in comparison to the United States. And so, the problem feeds upon itself.

The third reason for the EU's inability to challenge the United States is that the EU states suffer from an aging and changing workforce, and both elements have the potential to hobble its already slow economic growth. The major European economies of Britain, France, Germany, and Italy will need several million new workers over the next fifteen years to fill positions vacated by retiring ones. Presently, those workers do not exist because fewer European women are having children, and this "baby bust" ultimately will make it impossible to sustain the generous welfare benefits provided by European governments.

In fact, declining European birthrates are affecting Europe as profoundly as any event in the past, even the Black Death of the 1300s or the World Wars. Simply put, Europeans are not replacing themselves. Europe's total fertility rate is about 1.4, far below the 2.1 births per female necessary to sustain a population (what demographers call the replacement level). In fact, no Western European country has a replacement-level birthrate. In 2004, Germany's birthrate was 1.3, Italy's 1.2, Spain's 1.1, and France's 1.7 (and France's high birthrate was largely due to its Muslim population).[49] The difference between replacement-level birthrates and those of Germany, or Italy, or Spain is the difference between a stable population size and one that decreases by one-third with each generation. Nothing like this has occurred in Europe absent wars or plagues. It is truly without parallel in history.

Consequently, present welfare benefits are unsustainable given the population growth estimates for European states. In Europe, there are now thirty-five people of retirement age for every one hundred of working age and—based on current trends—there will be seventy-five pensioners for every one hundred workers—by 2050.[50] As Table 1.6 shows, the United Nations estimates that by 2015, Europe's population will decline by more than 11.3 million, and if Europe's current fertility rate persists until 2020, this will result in 88 million fewer Europeans by the end of the century.[51] Ethnic Europeans are dying out.

There are two major solutions to this problem, but they are unlikely to be realized. The first is to generate greater economic growth. Of course, this is easier said than done. Germany, the largest economy, has restrictive labor laws that are difficult to change. Another boost to economic growth would be to

Table 1.6 United Nations Population Estimates

Country	Population (in Millions, Medium Variant)			
	2000	2015	2025	2050
China	1,275	1,402	1,445	1,395
EU (25)[a]	452	457	456	431
France	59	63	64	64
Germany	82	82	82	79
India	1,017	1,246	1,369	1,531
Japan	127	127	123	110
Russia	146	133	124	101
United Kingdom	59	61	63	66
U.S.	285	330	358	409
World	6,070	7,197	7,851	8,918

Note: China excludes Hong Kong and Macao.

[a] EU (25): Austria, Belgium, Cyprus, Czech Republic, Denmark, Estonia, Finland, France, Germany, Greece, Hungary, Ireland, Italy, Latvia, Lithuania, Luxembourg, Malta, Netherlands, Poland, Portugal, Slovakia, Slovenia, Spain, Sweden, United Kingdom.

Source: Data from United Nations Population Division, *World Population Prospects: The 2002 Revision*, (New York: The United Nations, 2002).

reform their social welfare, education, and tax systems to encourage people to work longer hours and retire later. But, at this time, there is no indication that Europe will take these steps. Desire for change is not coming from the bottom up—the people are not demanding change in governmental polities because such a change would require sacrifice by present workers, pensioners, and other benefit recipients. Similarly, it is not coming from the top down—governments or Brussels imposing change—because this would require that leaders break their promises of protection to their populations.

Second, Europe could permit more legal immigration to provide workers, who then may be taxed to maintain welfare payments to Europe's aging population. However, most of the immigrants are likely to be Muslims coming from North Africa and the Middle East. Europe has had difficulty assimilating the Muslims it has already allowed into Europe, principally as workers beginning the 1960s, with a second wave coming in the 1980s as economic and political conditions deteriorated in North Africa. There are some 1 million Muslims in the Netherlands, 6 million in France, and about 13 million in the EU as a whole.

The different political and cultural practices of Muslim immigrants, whether they are old or new, are a quandary for Europe. The murder of Dutch filmmaker Theo van Gogh in November 2004 by a Muslim fundamentalist, who nonetheless had lived in the Netherlands for most of his life, was a great shock to Europe. In the Netherlands alone there have been constant threats by fundamentalists against other politicians like Geert Wilders, Amsterdam mayor Job Cohen, and Ayaan Hirsi Ali—a Somali-born member of parliament who collaborated with van Gogh on a film about Islam's treatment of women. Indeed, a December 2004 report by the Dutch domestic intelligence service concluded that many thousands of Muslim youths in the Netherlands are already radicalized, and thus the pool of recruits for terrorist actions is so large that many future attacks may be expected.[52] In October and November 2005, the widespread riots that plagued France in what has been called *l'intafada* by some or the beginning of the Eurabian civil war by others was conducted mostly by sons and grandsons of Muslim immigrants. The French were wholly unprepared for the scale and potency of the unrest and this caused them to fear a Muslim fifth column in Europe.

These threats and acts of violence point to the difficulty of matching the goals of European governments with the political realities of a young, Muslim population. Indeed, there are many Islamist movements operating and growing in Europe, including *al Qaeda* and *Al-Takfir wa al-Hijra* (excommunication and exile), a brutal terrorist organization active throughout Europe that is every bit as dangerous as *al Qaeda*.[53]

Consequently, there is a tension between sustaining European political and cultural values and economic growth based on a Muslim workforce that is becoming more conscious of the political goals of Islamic fundamentalism. As their numbers grow, so will the political power of Muslims in Europe. In a December 2004 report, the National Intelligence Council found that about fifteen out of one hundred Europeans are Muslims, and by 2020 it estimates that as many as thirty-five out of one hundred may be Muslim, or as few as twenty-three out of one hundred.[54] In either case, whether Muslims are one-third or one-quarter of the population or somewhere in between, it would mean a fundamental change in European society. If these trends do not change, Europe will have a Muslim majority population by the end of the twenty-first century.

Even if the EU solves its economic and immigration problems, it remains hindered by its cumbersome decision-making process that retards united and collective action. There are strong tensions between centralized decision making in Brussels and the respective capitals of the member states—Berlin, London, Madrid, Paris, or Rome. The interests of individual countries often do not overlap with Brussels's interests, and this is a major source of friction. Too much centralized decision making leads to a "democracy gap" in the EU—the key decision-making bodies in the EU are not directly elected by European citizens. In 2005, the overwhelming votes against the proposed EU Constitution in France and the Netherlands are indications of a major disconnect between Brussels and the European people. Increasingly, Europeans do not want to be told what to do by Brussels; Poland did not escape the grip of Moscow's leaders to have it replaced by those in Brussels. But too little central control leads to disorganization, repetition of efforts, and policy confusion.

Thus, for the EU to sustain positive growth rates—the numbers that would allow it to have an economy that could challenge the United States—it must steer between the Scylla of major economic, policy, and decision-making reforms and the Charybdis of Muslim immigration. Thus far, there is no evidence that the EU can conduct such a feat of navigation.

The Threat from Islamic Fundamentalist Terrorism: Dangerous but Manageable The terrorist attacks of 9/11 demonstrated the danger the terrorist group *al Qaeda* poses to the United States. In the wake of that attack, the United States launched Operation Enduring Freedom to overthrow the Taliban regime in Afghanistan, which sheltered *al Qaeda*, and to put great pressure on *al Qaeda*'s members and finances throughout the world. Great progress has been made in the war against *al Qaeda*. The United States has been successful at undermining that terrorist network, the Department of Homeland Security has been created to aid the defense of American territory, and, most importantly, no attacks have occurred on American soil since 9/11. But the war on terrorism is at root a war of ideas. As Secretary of Defense Rumsfeld explained in 2003, "all elements of national power: military, financial, diplomatic, law enforcement, intelligence and public diplomacy," are necessary to win the war on terror. But, he added, "to win the war on terror, we must also win the war of ideas." Military, diplomatic, and other elements are necessary "to stop terrorists before they can terrorize," but "even better, we must lean forward and stop them from becoming terrorists in the first place."[55] Winning the war of ideas is critical to keeping people from becoming terrorists.

Americans need to remember that their country has fought and won wars of ideas before. World War II was a war of ideas between liberalism and fascism. The Cold War took the war of ideas to new heights. Few Americans comprehend how attractive communism was in a Europe destroyed by World War II. Communism seemed to offer a better life and, in many countries, such as France and Italy, the communists had a solid record of fighting the Germans. Nonetheless, the United States engaged communism in a war of ideas and won.

It can also win the physical battle with the few extremists in the Islamic world who are motivated by a contorted fundamentalist interpretation of Islam. The majority of Muslims are not fundamentalists, and in fact reject fundamentalism as simply wrong. Leading Sunni scholars have stigmatized fundamentalism as aberrant—a perversion of the religion. Even to most Muslims who are fundamentalists, *al Qaeda* is seen as a deviant group that is wrong to use terrorism as a weapon against innocent civilians, including their coreligionists (many of *al Qaeda*'s victims have been Muslim), governments in the Islamic world, and the West.

To combat *al Qaeda*, the United States must take the following actions. First, it has to stress that the war on terrorism is not conducted by the West against Muslims, but is a struggle between *al Qaeda*, which wants to take the Muslim world into the twelfth century, and those who want to bring it into the twenty-first. Americans must realize that we have many allies in the Muslim world. Like the Cold War, the war against terrorism is not a war we fight alone. The United States has many allies not only in Europe and northeast Asia, like Japan but, more importantly for this struggle, it has numerous allies in the Muslim world. In fact, when one examines the U.S. allies in the region, what is remarkable is the amount of support that Washington has among the governments in the Middle East. The major allies of the United States at the end of the Cold War remain—Egypt, Israel, Saudi Arabia, and Turkey are strong allies. Moreover, from Morocco to the Gulf, most of the smaller states in the Arab world are allied with the United States. Jordan is a reliable ally, as is Morocco. This provides the United States with a powerful foundation from which to exert influence within and outside of the Middle East. Even Libya has made a dramatic about-face. In 2003, it renounced its weapons of mass destruction program and now is changing from being one of the most anti-American countries to one that is beginning to support the United States and the West as it seeks to integrate into the global economy. Indeed, of all the states in the Middle East, only Iran and Syria remain outside the orb of U.S. influence. From Morocco to Indonesia, the vast majority of the countries of the Arab and, more broadly, Muslim world are allied with the United States.

Second, the United States must have the will to conduct this war. It will be a long conflict with setbacks, including other terrorist attacks against American targets at home and abroad. The American people need to be steeled for a long campaign—one that George W. Bush will pass on to his successor, and the one after that. There were nine U.S. presidents during the Cold War, and we should expect a like number in this campaign.

To its credit, the administration is taking many of the right steps and has labored assiduously to place pressure on *al Qaeda* as rapidly as possible to weaken it. It has evicted *al Qaeda* from its training camps in Afghanistan and labored to cut off *al Qaeda*'s considerable financial resources. It is attempting to extinguish all of the known cells at once, from Germany to Kenya to Malaysia, by placing pressure on the governments.

There will be no quick and easy victory against *al Qaeda* and its related and spin-off terrorist groups, but there will be victory. It will not be like the end of World War II, where there was a surrender ceremony on the decks of the USS *Missouri*; this does not happen when terrorist groups are defeated—they usually just wither away. This might happen as terrorist organizations splinter into impotence and gradually die as the social and political conditions in the Muslim world change, making *al Qaeda* and similar groups political dinosaurs in the age of mammals. Or perhaps—much like the Provisional IRA—former terrorists could melt into established political life of some countries in the Islamic world.

The American victory in the war against *al Qaeda* begins by recognizing that terrorist organizations not only can be defeated but, indeed, often are. Almost all of the left-wing terrorist organizations of the Cold War were defeated—from the Weather Underground in the United States to the Japanese Red Army, the Red Army faction in Germany, and the Red Brigades in Italy. The Peruvians defeated the Shining Path. The British fought the IRA to a standstill. The French defeated Corsican nationalists and the communist terrorist group Direct Action. The Algerians have successfully suppressed the Armed Islamic Group (GIA), an especially vicious terrorist organization that killed well over one hundred thousand people between 1990 and 2000 in Algeria and France.[56] In 1994, a GIA terrorist thankfully was thwarted from flying an Air France aircraft into the Eiffel Tower—an attack that served as a template for the 9/11 attacks in the United States. Spain has greatly weakened the Basque separatist terrorist group ETA. The Turks have emasculated the PKK (now called New PKK). The Israelis defeated the PLO, as did the Jordanians. And while the Israelis have not destroyed the three major terrorist groups, Fatah, Hamas, and Palestinian Islamic Jihad, they have been extremely effective at penetrating these groups to prevent attacks. Attacks have declined 60 percent between 2003 and 2004—there were only six suicide bombings in Israel and eight in the occupied territories—and the Israelis believe they foiled 114 planned suicide bombings in 2004.[57] Reflecting on the decline of these groups over the last few years, the Israel internal security organization, Shin Bet, estimates that it prevents 90 percent of attacks before they occur. The Egyptians have broken the back of the Islamic Group and of Egyptian Islamic Jihad. So while it is true that *al Qaeda* should not be underestimated—it is motivated, competent, and resilient—it does have vulnerabilities and can be defeated, just as many terrorist groups before it were.

Should America Dominate the World? Yes, It Is a Force for Good in the World and Far Better than Any Realistic Alternative

A great amount of good comes from American dominance, although that good is little acknowledged, even by Americans. In this section, I will demonstrate the good that comes from the American Empire. Specifically, it provides stability, allows democracy to spread, furthers economic prosperity, and makes possible humanitarian assistance to countries beset by natural and other disasters. The United States has an opportunity to do an enormous amount of good for itself and the entire world. Realizing this good requires that Americans be bold, that they lead. In return, Americans enjoy the benefits that flow to a leader.

But as professors teach in Economics 101, there is no free lunch. No one gets anything for free; everything has a cost. The American Empire is no exception. I want to make it clear that the benefits that the world and the United States enjoy come with a cost. Leadership requires that the United States incur costs and run risks not borne by other countries. These costs can be stark and brutal, and they have to be faced directly by proponents of the American Empire. It means that some Americans will die in the service of their country. These are the costs. They are considerable. Every American should be conscious of them. It is equally the case that Americans should be aware of the benefits they enjoy. I believe that the substantial benefits are worth the costs.

Stability

Peace, like good health, is not often noticed, but certainly is missed when absent. Throughout history, peace and stability have been a major benefit of empires. In fact, *pax Romana* in Latin means the Roman peace, or the stability brought about by the Roman Empire. Rome's power was so overwhelming that no one could challenge it successfully for hundreds of years. The result was stability within the Roman Empire. Where Rome conquered, peace, law, order, education, a common language, and much else followed. That was true of the British Empire (*pax Britannica*) too.

So it is with the United States today. Peace and stability are major benefits of the American Empire. The fact that America is so powerful actually reduces the likelihood of major war. Scholars of international politics have found that the presence of a dominant state in international politics actually reduces the likelihood of war because weaker states, including even great powers, know that it is unlikely that they could challenge the dominant state and win. They may resort to other mechanisms or tactics to challenge the dominant country, but are unlikely to do so directly. This means that there will be no wars between great powers. At least, not until a challenger (certainly China) thinks it can overthrow the dominant state (the United States). But there will be intense security competition—both China and the United States will watch each other closely, with their intelligence communities increasingly focused on each other, their diplomats striving to ensure that countries around the world do not align with the other, and their militaries seeing the other as their principal threat. This is not unusual in international politics but, in fact, is its "normal" condition. Americans may not pay much attention to it until a crisis occurs. But right now states are competing with one another. This is because international politics does not sleep; it never takes a rest.

Spreading Our Form of Government

The American Empire gives the United States the ability to spread its form of government, democracy, and other elements of its ideology of liberalism. Using American power to spread democracy can be a source of much good for the countries concerned as well as for the United States. This is because democracies are more likely to align themselves with the United States and be sympathetic to its worldview. In addition, there is a chance—small as it may be—that once states are governed democratically, the likelihood of conflict will be reduced further. Natan Sharansky makes the argument that once Arabs are governed democratically, they will not wish to continue the conflict against Israel.[58] This idea has had a big effect on President George W. Bush. He has said that Sharansky's worldview "is part of my presidential DNA."[59]

Whether democracy in the Middle East would have this impact is debatable. Perhaps democratic Arab states would be more opposed to Israel, but nonetheless, their people would be better off. The United States has brought democracy to Afghanistan, where 8.5 million Afghans, 40 percent of them women, voted in October 2004, even though remnant Taliban forces threatened them. Elections were held in Iraq in January 2005, the first free elections in that country's history. The military power of the United States put Iraq on the path to democracy. Democracy has spread to Latin America, Europe, Asia, the Caucasus, and now even the Middle East is becoming increasingly democratic. They may not yet look like Western-style democracies, but democratic progress has been made in Morocco, Lebanon, Iraq, Kuwait, the Palestinian Authority, and Egypt. The march of democracy has been impressive.

Although democracies have their flaws, simply put, democracy is the best form of government. Winston Churchill recognized this over half a century ago: "Democracy is the worst form of government except all those other forms that have been tried from time to time." The United States should do what it can to foster the spread of democracy throughout the world.

Economic Prosperity

Economic prosperity is also a product of the American Empire. It has created a Liberal International Economic Order (LIEO)—a network of worldwide free trade and commerce, respect for intellectual property rights, mobility of capital and labor markets—to promote economic growth. The stability and prosperity that stems from this economic order is a global public good from which all states benefit, particularly states in the Third World. The American Empire has created this network not out of altruism but because it benefits the economic well-being of the United States. In 1998, the Secretary of Defense William Cohen put this well when he acknowledged that "economists and soldiers share the same interest in stability"; soldiers create the conditions in which the American economy may thrive, and "we are able to shape the environment [of international politics] in ways that are advantageous to us and that are stabilizing to the areas where we are forward deployed, thereby helping to promote investment and prosperity...business follows the flag."[60]

Perhaps the greatest testament to the benefits of the American Empire comes from Deepak Lal, a former Indian foreign service diplomat, researcher at the World Bank, prolific author, and now a professor who started his career confident in the socialist ideology of post-independence India that strongly condemned empire. He has abandoned the position of his youth and is now one of the strongest proponents of the American Empire. Lal has traveled the world and, in the course of his journeys, has witnessed great poverty and misery due to a lack of economic development. He realized that free markets were necessary for the development of poor countries, and this led him to recognize that his faith in socialism was wrong. Just as a conservative famously is said to be a liberal who has been mugged by reality, the hard "evidence and experience" that stemmed from "working and traveling in most parts of the Third World during my professional career" caused this profound change.[61]

Lal submits that the only way to bring relief to the desperately poor countries of the Third World is through the American Empire. Empires provide order, and this order "has been essential for the working of the benign processes of globalization, which promote prosperity."[62] Globalization is the process of creating a common economic space, which leads to a growing integration of the world economy through the increasingly free movement of goods, capital, and labor. It is the responsibility of the United States, Lal argues, to use the LIEO to promote the well-being of all economies, but particularly those in the Third World, so that they too may enjoy economic prosperity.

Humanitarian Missions

If someone were to ask "How many humanitarian missions has the United States undertaken since the end of the Cold War?", most Americans probably have to think for a moment and then answer "three or four." In fact, the number is much larger. The U.S. military has participated in over fifty operations since the end of the Cold War, and while wars like the invasion of Panama or Iraq received considerable attention from the world's media, most of the fifty actions were humanitarian in nature and received almost no media attention in the United States.

The U.S. military is the earth's "911 force"—it serves as the world's police; it is the global paramedic, and the planet's fire department. Whenever there is a natural disaster, earthquake, flood, typhoon, or tsunami, the United States assists the countries in need. In 1991, when flooding caused by cyclone Marian killed almost 140,000 people and left 5 million homeless in Bangladesh, the United States launched Operation Sea Angel to save stranded and starving people by supplying food, potable water, and medical assistance. U.S. forces are credited with saving over 200,000 lives in that operation.

In 1999, torrential rains and flash flooding in Venezuela killed 30,000 people and left 140,000 homeless. The United States responded with Operation Fundamental Response, which brought water purification and hygiene equipment saving thousands. Also in 1999, Operation Strong Support aided Central Americans affected by Hurricane Mitch. That hurricane was the fourth-strongest ever recorded in the Atlantic and the worst natural disaster to strike Central America in the twentieth century. The magnitude of the devastation was tremendous, with about 10,000 people killed, 13,000 missing, and 2 million left homeless. It is estimated that 60 percent of the infrastructure in Honduras, Nicaragua, and Guatemala was destroyed. Again, the U.S. military came to the aid of the people affected. It is believed to have rescued about 700 people who otherwise would have died, while saving more from disease due to the timely arrival of medical supplies, food, water, blankets, and mobile shelters. In the next phase of Strong Support, military engineers rebuilt much of the infrastructure of those countries, including bridges, hospitals, roads, and schools.

On the day after Christmas in 2004, a tremendous earthquake and tsunami occurred in the Indian Ocean near Sumatra and killed 300,000 people. The United States was the first to respond with aid. More importantly, Washington not only contributed a large amount of aid, $350 million, plus another $350 million provided by American citizens and corporations, but also—only days after the tsunami struck—used its military to help those in need. About 20,000 U.S. soldiers, sailors, airmen, and marines responded by providing water, food, medical aid, disease treatment and prevention, as well as forensic assistance to help identify the bodies of those killed. Only the U.S. military could have accomplished this Herculean effort, and it is important to keep in mind that its costs were separate from the $350 million provided by the U.S. government and other money given by American citizens and corporations to relief organizations like the International Committee of the Red Cross/Red Crescent.

The generosity of the United States has done more to help the country fight the war on terror than almost any other measure. Before the tsunami, 80 percent of Indonesian opinion was opposed to the United States; after it, 80 percent had a favorable opinion of the United States. In October 2005, an enormous earthquake struck Kashmir, killing about 74,000 people and leaving 3 million homeless. The U.S. military responded immediately, diverting helicopters fighting the war on terror in nearby Afghanistan to bring relief as soon as possible. To help those in need, the United States provided about $156 million in aid to Pakistan; and, as one might expect from those witnessing the generosity of the United States, it left a lasting impression about the United States. Whether in Indonesia or Kashmir, the money was well spent because it helped people in the wake of disasters, but it also had a real impact on the war on terror.

There is no other state or international organization that can provide these benefits. The United Nations certainly cannot because it lacks the military and economic power of the United States. It is riven with conflicts and major cleavages that divide the international body time and again on small matters as well as great ones. Thus, it lacks the ability to speak with one voice on important issues and to act as a unified force once a decision has been reached. Moreover, it does not possess the communications capabilities or global logistical reach of the U.S. military. In fact, UN peacekeeping operations depend on the United States to supply UN forces. Simply put, there is no alternative to the leadership of the United States.

When the United States does not intervene, as it has not in the Darfur region of Sudan and eastern Chad, people die. In this conflict, Arab Muslims belonging to government forces, or a militia called the Jingaweit, are struggling against Christian and animist black Africans who are fighting for independence. According to the State Department, 98,000 to 181,000 people died between March 2003 and March 2005 as a result of this struggle. The vast majority of these deaths were caused by violence, disease, and malnutrition associated with the conflict.

Conclusion

The American Empire is fully in keeping with the Founding Fathers' dreams for America. America has never been a shrinking violet, hiding from the world. Rather, it has been a bold country, making a place for itself in international politics since its inception. The empire Americans have worked hard to create can last well into the future, but only if the American people want it to persevere. As I have argued in this chapter, the American Empire should be valued by the American people largely because of the enormous good it does for America and the honorable and goodhearted actions it undertakes for the world. It is equally true that this good is not often appreciated by the rest of the world, or sometimes even in the United States.

Despite its benefits, Americans have to recognize that they will be criticized, and that this is simply a consequence of its power. A half a century ago, the great British historian Arnold Toynbee hit this point precisely when he wrote of American power: "The giant's sheer size is always getting the giant into trouble with people of normal stature."[63] Toynbee writes of a Latin American diplomat who captured the point well: "When the United States sneezes, Latin America gets influenza."[64] Its actions will always have an exaggerated impact on smaller countries. And that fact alone will generate resentment and jealously from those who are weaker.

No matter what, people will launch invective against the United States. Muslims will attack it as too atheistic and hedonistic; Europeans will assault it from the opposite direction, labeling the United States as too religious and crude. Mark Steyn, the witty columnist for the *Daily Telegraph*, wrote with great insight:

> Fanatical Muslims despise America because it's all lapdancing and gay
> porn; the secular Europeans despise America because it's all born-again

Christians hung up on abortion....America is also too isolationist, except when it is too imperialist. And even its imperialism is too vulgar and arriviste to appeal to real imperialists....To the mullahs, America is the Great Satan, a wily seducer; to the Gaullists, America is the Great Cretin, a culture so self-evidently moronic that only stump-tooth inbred Appalachian lardbutts could possibly fall for it....Too Christian, too Godless, too isolationist, too imperialist, too seductive, too cretinous.[65]

The key question for the future is not how Muslims, Europeans, or others will perceive the American Empire. Rather, it is "How should Americans want our empire to be remembered?" As one that fostered democracy in places where freedom was unknown—from Afghanistan and Iraq to Chile and Argentina to Germany and Japan. As one that developed respect for free market values and institutionalized these values in organizations like the World Trade Organization. Did it make mistakes? Of course, it did. Did Americans have to sacrifice their lives? Unfortunately, many did. But when the sun sets on the American Empire, we will acknowledge that the world was the better for having it.

More reading

Notes

1. Authors who are proponents of isolationism include Ted Galen Carpenter, *A Search for Enemies: America's Alliances after the Cold War* (Washington, D.C.: Cato Institute, 1992); Ivan Eland, *The Empire Has No Clothes: U.S. Foreign Policy Exposed* (Oakland, Calif.: The Independent Institute, 2004); Eugene Gholz, Daryl G. Press, and Harvey M. Sapolsky, "Come Home, America: The Strategy of Restraint in the Face of Temptation," *International Security* 21 (4): 5–48.
2. See, for example, Robert J. Art, "Geopolitics Updated: The Strategy of Selective Engagement," *International Security* 23 (3): 79–113; Stephen Van Evera, "Why Europe Matters, Why the Third World Doesn't: American Grand Strategy after the Cold War," *The Journal of Strategic Studies* 13 (2): 1–51. Christopher Layne argues for a grand strategy of "offshore balancing," which is related conceptually to selective engagement, although the policies derived from it may be substantially different from selective engagement. Christopher Layne, "From Preponderance to Offshore Balancing: America's Future Grand Strategy," *International Security* 22 (1): 86–124.
3. Key articles making this argument include: Andrew J. Bacevich, *American Empire: The Realities and Consequences of U.S. Diplomacy* (Cambridge, Mass.: Harvard University Press, 2002); Samuel P. Huntington, "Why International Primacy Matters," *International Security* 17 (4): 68–83; William C. Wohlforth, "The Stability of a Unipolar World," *International Security* 24 (1): 5–41. Also see Charles Krauthammer, "The Unipolar Moment," *Foreign Affairs* 70 (1): 23–33. For the argument that primacy or "preponderance" motivated the grand strategy of the United States at the beginning of the Cold War see Melvyn P. Leffler, *A Preponderance of Power: National Security, the Truman Administration, and the Cold War* (Stanford, Calif.: Stanford University Press, 1992).
4. My definition of empire is heavily influenced by George Liska's exceptional study of the American empire. His book is as relevant now as when it was written over a generation ago. See Liska, *Imperial America: The International Politics of Primacy* (Baltimore: Johns Hopkins Press, 1967), pp. 9–10.
5. Joseph S. Nye Jr., *Soft Power: The Means to Success in World Politics* (New York: Public Affairs, 2004), p. x.
6. John C. Fitzpatrick, ed., *The Writings of George Washington* (Washington, D.C.: Government Printing Office, 1938), Vol. 28, p. 520.

7. For a comprehensive discussion of Jefferson's view of the United States in the world see Robert W. Tucker and David C. Hendrickson, *Empire of Liberty: The Statecraft of Thomas Jefferson* (New York: Oxford University Press, 1990). On September 19, 1803, Jefferson characterized the United States as an "empire for liberty" in a missive to Andrew Jackson. See Adrienne Koch, *Jefferson and Madison: The Great Collaboration* (New York: Alfred A. Knopf, 1950), p. 244. Jefferson's 1805 remarks about the United States as "a chosen country" and "rising nation" are quoted in Anders Stephanson, *Manifest Destiny: American Expansion and the Empire of Right* (New York: Hill and Wang, 1995), p. 21.

8. Jefferson to James Madison, April 27, 1809, from *The Thomas Jefferson Papers Series 1: General Correspondence 1651–1827*, Library of Congress, image 1110.

9. Thomas Paine, *Rights of Man* (Mineola, N.Y.: Dover Publications, 1999), Part II, p. 145.

10. Reginald C. Stuart, *United States Expansionism and British North America, 1775–1871* (Chapel Hill: The University of North Carolina Press, 1988), p. 13. Stuart quotes correspondence from George Mason to Richard Henry Lee on July 21, 1778. What is particularly interesting about it is that it is typically American. America's security requires complete dominance: "The Union is yet incomplete, and will be so, until the inhabitants of all the territory from Cape Breton to the Mississippi are included in it: while Great Britain possesses Canada and West Florida, she will be continually setting the Indians upon us, and while she holds the harbors of Augustine and Halifax, especially the latter, we shall not be able to protect our trade or coasts from her depredations." Stuart, *United States Expansionism and British North America, 1775–1871*, p. 8.

11. In an exceptional book, Fred Anderson and Andrew Cayton, eminent scholars of American history, submit that while many citizens believe the expansion of their country's power was done for defensive reasons; e.g., defending American liberty, the historical reality is that the expansion occurred due to the desire to expand American power. See Anderson and Cayton, *The Dominion of War: Empire and Liberty in North America 1500–2000* (New York: Viking, 2005).

12. See Warren Zimmermann, *The First Great Triumph: How Five Americans Made Their Country a World Power* (New York: Farrar, Straus and Giroux, 2002).

13. Charles Francis Adams, ed., *Memoirs of John Quincy Adams* (New York: AMS Press, 1970), Vol. 4, p. 438.

14. Adam Smith, *An Inquiry into the Nature and Causes of the Wealth of Nations* (New York: Modern Library, 1937), pp. 587–588.

15. Alexis de Tocqueville, *Democracy in America*, trans. George Lawrence (New York: Harper Perennial, 1988), Vol. 1, pp. 412–413.

16. Felix Gilbert, *To the Farewell Address: Ideas of Early American Foreign Policy* (Princeton, N.J.: Princeton University Press, 1961), p. 72.

17. I assume, of course, that no completely unexpected catastrophe occurs—massive earthquakes, volcanic eruptions, a terrible epidemic, or some other event—that would greatly damage the United States and destroy its ability to maintain its preponderance.

18. In fiscal year (October 1–September 30) 2005 it spent approximately $400 billion, and in fiscal year 2006, about $420 billion. This figure does not count supplemental appropriations to fight the War on Terrorism or the war in Iraq. From initial deployments of troops in the fall and winter of 2002 through the end of fiscal year 2004 (September 30, 2004), the United States spent $102 billion in Iraq, at an average cost of $4.8 billion a month. If the spending of other governmental agencies, such as the CIA, is included, the amount would be greater, probably by several billion dollars. The United States spent $39.8 billion in Afghanistan from the October 2001 invasion to overthrow the Taliban government until September 30, 2004.

19. Newt Gingrich, "Remarks Delivered at the Center for Strategic and International Studies," quoted in Ivan Eland, *The Empire Has No Clothes* (Oakland, Calif.: The Independent Institute, 2004), p. 184.

20. Steven Kosiak, "Historical and Projected Funding for Defense: Presentation of the FY 2005 Request in Tables and Charts," Center for Strategic and Budgetary Assessments, February 2004, Table 2.

21. Deputy Secretary Wolfowitz Interview with Tempo, United States Department of Defense, Sunday, January 16, 2005, http://dod.mil/transcripts/2004/tr20050116-depsecdef1986.html.

22. Barry R. Posen, "Command of the Commons: The Military Foundation of U.S. Hegemony," *International Security* 28 (1): 5–46.

23. Deputy Secretary of Defense Paul Wolfowitz, "Deputy Secretary Wolfowitz Holds Joint Press Conference in Indonesia," Jakarta, Indonesia, January 16, 2005, http://www.defenselink.mil/transcripts/2005/tr20050116-depsecdef1989.html.
24. Ibid.
25. An excellent overview of NATO's crises during the Cold War as well as its post–Cold War missions is provided by Lawrence S. Kaplan, *NATO Divided, NATO United: The Evolution of an Alliance* (New York: Praeger, 2004).
26. Data are drawn from the CIA's World Factbook. GDP for European Union member states is drawn from the European Union: http://www.cia.gov/cia/publications/factbook/geos/ee.html; and for the United States: http://www.cia.gov/cia/publications/factbook/geos/us.html. The fact that the U.S. estimate is a year behind may actually mean that in 2004 the United States had a larger economy given that the CIA estimates the EU had a 1 percent real growth rate and the United States had a 3.1 percent real growth rate in 2003, which means that the economies are the same size.
27. Niall Ferguson, "Our Currency, Your Problem," *New York Times Sunday Magazine*, 13 March 2005, http://www.nytimes.com/2005/03/13/magazine/13WWLN.html.
28. Ibid.
29. Michael E. Porter, et al., *The Global Competitiveness Report 2004–2005* (Geneva: World Economic Forum, 2004), p. xii.
30. Deepak Lal, *In Praise of Empires: Globalization and Order* (New York: Palgrave Macmillan, 2004), p. 69. Emphasis in original.
31. Porter, et al., *The Global Competitiveness Report 2004–2005*, p. 154.
32. Paul Kennedy, "Empire without 'Overstretch'," *Wilson Quarterly* 26 (3), online edition.
33. Ibid.
34. Each of these problems is delineated and solutions are offered in *Report of the Defense Science Board Task Force on Strategic Communication* (Washington, D.C.: Office of the Under Secretary of Defense for Acquisition, Technology, and Logistics, Department of Defense, 2004).
35. Powell is quoted by Joseph S. Nye Jr., "You Can't Get Here from There," *The New York Times*, November 29, 2004, online edition.
36. Oleg Kalugin recounts his experience as a KGB agent posing as a student in *Spymaster: The Highest-Ranking KGB Officer Ever to Break His Silence* (London: Smith Gryphon, 1994).
37. Joyce Howard Price, "World Speaks Our Language and Attends Our Colleges," *The Washington Times*, December 29, 2004, online edition.
38. Although film and television are wonderful popular entertainment, Americans and others often forget that America is the home to 1,700 symphony orchestras, 7.5 million people attend the opera each year, and 500 million people visit America's museums.
39. David R. Sands, "America Enjoys View from the Top," *Washington Times*, 27 December 2004, online edition.
40. Simon Schama, "The Unloved American," *New Yorker*, 10 March 2003, online edition at: http://www.newyorker.com/printable/?/fact/030310fa_fact.
41. A particularly insightful study of how American consumer culture has spread throughout the world is Victoria de Grazia, *Irresistible Empire: America's Advance through 20th-Century Europe* (Cambridge, Mass.: The Belknap Press of Harvard University Press, 2005).
42. The 8 percent estimates are from the Central Intelligence Agency, *The World Factbook—China*, www.cia.gov/cia/publications/factbook/geos/ch.html. The 2001 estimate is from the U.S. Department of Energy's Energy Information Agency, "Country Analysis Briefs—China," June 2002 at http://www.eia.doe.gov/cabs/china.html.
43. National Intelligence Council, *Mapping the Global Future: Report of the National Intelligence Council's 2020 Project* (Washington, D.C.: National Intelligence Council, 2004), p. 32.
44. Ching-Ching Ni, "China Confronts Its Daunting Gender Gap," *New York Times*, 21 January 2005, online edition.
45. T.R. Reid, *The United States of Europe: The New Superpower and the End of American Supremacy* (New York: Penguin Press, 2004), p. 87.
46. Samuel P. Huntington, *The Clash of Civilizations and the Remaking of World Order* (New York: Simon & Schuster, 1996).
47. Reid, *The United States of Europe*, p. 288n2.
48. Reid, *The United States of Europe*, p. 155.

49. George Weigel, *The Cube and the Cathedral: Europe, America, and Politics without God* (New York: Basic Books, 2005), pp. 21–22.

50. Phillip Longman, *The Empty Cradle: How Falling Birthrates Threaten World Prosperity and What to Do About It* (New York: Basic Books, 2004), pp. 62–63

51. Ibid., pp. 62, 67.

52. Menno Steketee, "Dutch Authorities Report Increase in Islamist Radicalisation," *Jane's Intelligence Review* 17 (2): 20–21.

53. Tamara Makarenko, "Takfiri Presence Grows in Europe," *Jane's Intelligence Review* 17 (2): 16–19. Other Islamic fundamentalist terrorist groups operating in Europe include the Armed Islamic Group, the Libyan Fighting Islamic Group, the Moroccan Islamic Combatant Group, the Salafist Group for Preaching and Combat, the Tunisian Combatant Group, and the Tunisian Islamic Front.

54. National Intelligence Council, *Mapping the Global Future*, p. 83.

55. Donald R. Rumsfeld, "Take the Fight to the Terrorists," *Washington Post*, 26 October 2003, p. B7.

56. The GIA specialized in mass killings. For example, in Bin Talha, a suburb of Algiers, they cut the throats of some eight hundred people, mostly women and children, in a single night. But they were also expert at conducting assassinations, including those of the president and its most important trade union leader.

57. Nina Gilbert, "IDF: Significant Decline in 2004 Terror," *The Jerusalem Post*, 22 December 2004, http://www.jpost.com/servlet/Satellite?pagename=JPost/JPArticle/ShowFull&cid=1103602489600&p=1078027574097.

58. Natan Sharansky with Ron Dermer, *The Case for Democracy: The Power of Freedom to Overcome Tyranny and Terror* (New York: Public Affairs, 2004).

59. Caroline Glick, "Column One: The Sharansky Moment?" *The Jerusalem Post*, 3 March 2005, http://www.jpost.com/servlet/Satellite?pagename=Jpost/ShowFull&cid=11098200 04306&p=1006953079897.

60. Bacevich, *American Empire*, p. 128.

61. Lal, *In Praise of Empires*, pp. xv–xvi.

62. Ibid., p. xix.

63. Arnold J. Toynbee, *America and the World Revolution* (New York: Oxford University Press, 1962), pp. 208–209.

64. Ibid., p. 209.

65. Mark Steyn, "It's 'Peace' Psychosis in a Nut's Hell," *Daily Telegraph*, 18 November 2003, http://opinion.telegraph.co.uk/opinion/main.jhtml?xml=/opinion/2003/11/18/do1802.xml.

2

The Case Against the American Empire

CHRISTOPHER LAYNE

Introduction

The Issues

Since the Cold War's end, the United States has dominated international politics. It is—as international relations scholars put it—a "global hegemon." Indeed, in recent years in books and articles about U.S. foreign policy it has become commonplace to see the United States described as the most powerful actor on the international stage since the Roman Empire was at its zenith. This doubtless is true. The central question I address is whether the United States should seek to maintain its current primacy in world politics and use this preeminence to construct a new American Empire. At first blush, this may seem an odd question to ask. After all, since the ancient Greek historian Thucydides wrote his classic *History of the Peloponnesian War*, realists have understood that international politics is fundamentally about power. If this is true—and it is—how can it be argued that the United States might possess *too much* power for its own good?

The events of the last five years suggest the answer. In the aftermath of 9/11, Americans—citizens and policy-makers alike—asked repeatedly, "Why do they hate us?" President George W. Bush answered by claiming that the United States was the target of *al Qaeda*'s terrorist strikes because radical Islamicists hate America's freedom. More thoughtful analysts have pointed out that it is U.S. policies in the Middle East and Persian Gulf that caused the terrorists to attack the United States. In March 2003, the United States invaded Iraq. In this endeavor it was opposed not only by Russia and China, but also by long-time allies like Germany and France. Around the world, public opinion—which largely had been sympathetic to the United States in 9/11's wake—turned sharply against the United States. Increasingly, the United States has come to be perceived globally as an 800-pound gorilla on steroids—out of control, and dangerous to others. Far from being regarded as a "benevolent hegemon," America has come to be seen as a kind of global Lone Ranger, indifferent to its allies, ignoring international institutions like the United Nations, and acting in defiance of international law and norms. In the last five years there have been many indications that, far from welcoming American primacy, others worry about it—and sometimes find it downright threatening to their own interests and security. In other words, a too-powerful America risks a global geopolitical backlash against its preeminent position in international politics.

The issue of whether a strategy of primacy is good for the United States has been a subject of debate in the foreign policy community for the last fifteen years. After 9/11, however, the debate about primacy merged with another debate. Cognizant of America's overwhelming "hard" (military and economic) power, and believing in the attractiveness of its democratic values and institutions ("soft power"), some in the foreign policy community—mostly neoconservatives—urged that the United States should use its primacy to construct a new American Empire. The United States, it was urged, should use its hard and soft power to intervene in failed states like Afghanistan, and rogue states like Iraq, and engage in a policy of "nation-building" to ensure that such states no longer could serve as either terrorist havens or sources of instability and aggression. Writing in *The Weekly Standard* shortly after 9/11, the neoconservative pundit Max Boot argued that the United States should follow in Britain's imperial footsteps and administer Afghanistan—ruled by the Islamic fundamentalist Taliban, and home base to Osama Bin Laden and *al Qaeda*—until "a responsible, humane, preferably democratic government takes over."[1] Once the United States dealt with Afghanistan, the United States, Boot said, should invade Iraq and remove Saddam Hussein from power. As Boot freely admitted, the United States should do this even if Saddam Hussein was not implicated in the 9/11 attacks: "Who cares if Saddam was involved in this particular barbarity?"[2] By overthrowing Saddam Hussein the United States could "establish the first Arab democracy...[and] turn Iraq into a beacon of hope for the oppressed peoples of the Middle East."[3] The Bush II administration—the key national security positions of which were staffed by neoconservatives and neocon fellow-travelers—took up Boot's challenge. The March 2003 invasion of Iraq was the first step in the administration's "generational commitment" to bring about a "democratic transformation" in the Middle East.

The heart of the current debate about the direction of American foreign policy—about the costs and benefits of primacy and empire—is about security. Do primacy and empire make the United States more secure, or—as I argue—less secure? This debate is important not just for policy-makers, and foreign policy scholars, but also for *citizens*. The events of 9/11 underscored that the debate over America's grand strategy it not an abstract one. The policies the United States follows in the international arena have real-life consequences for Americans. To understand the debate about American primacy and empire, one must engage with the key theories of international politics that underlie both current U.S. strategy and its alternative, offshore balancing; and with competing narratives—that is, contrasting ideas about, and interpretations of—concerning America's proper role in world affairs. These narratives are rooted deeply in this nation's history and its political culture.

This may seem like a daunting challenge. After all, most Americans do not make their living studying international politics and U.S. foreign policy. But the challenge is not insuperable. The major debates about American foreign policy during the last six decades have reflected parallel debates in academe about "how the world works." These scholarly debates invariably seep into the real world of policy making and influence decision-makers' actions. After all, as leading scholars of strategic studies like Stephen Walt and Barry Posen have pointed out, far from being esoteric, grand strategy actually is policy-makers' theory of how to "cause" security for the United States. Put another way, decision-makers have a set of a cause and effect—or "if...then"—hypotheses about what policies will make the United States more—or less—secure. For example, American primacy and empire are based on—among others—two key propositions derived from international relations theory: that attaining, and keeping, overwhelming hard power—that is, primacy—is the strategy best calculated to ensure U.S. security; and that the United States should promote regime change abroad, because a world composed of democracies will be more stable and peaceful than a world in which "rogue states" are allowed to exist (a proposition derived from so-called democratic peace theory).

American grand strategy is shaped not only by theories of international politics and by the "balance of power," but also by *ideas*. Since the very founding of the Republic, the question of what America's "purpose" in international politics should be has been contested. There have been recurring controversies about how deeply the United States needs to be engaged in international politics in order to gain security and about whether engagement abroad strengthens or weakens America domestically. Indeed, the very term "security" has been a subject of contention. For the United States, is security determined by power relationships and geography (the traditional criteria that great powers have employed in determining their strategies), or can the United States be secure only in a world that shares its liberal democratic ideology? In the wake of 9/11, Americans once again have occasion to confront these enduring questions.

Michael Hunt has observed that American history has been marked by the clash of two contending visions of America's proper role in the world. One of these holds "that the American pursuit of lofty ambitions abroad, far from imperiling liberty, would serve to invigorate it at home, while creating conditions favorable to its spread in foreign lands."[4] This belief that America's mission is to remake the world in its image underlies the Bush II administration's pursuit of an American Empire. However, this expansive vision of America's world role has always existed side by side with a very different viewpoint, which has argued that America's political institutions, prosperity, and social cohesion are best safeguarded by a policy of restraint in foreign affairs. Proponents of this vision have "argued that the pursuit of greatness diverted attention and resources from real problems at home and might under some circumstances even aggravate or compound those problems. Foreign crusades unavoidably diminished national ideals and well being."[5]

Michael Hogan has elaborated on the way in which the two competing worldviews depicted by Hunt have influenced debates about American grand strategy since the end of World War II. One school of thought has believed in limited government at home and a limited role abroad. Those who cleaved to this view of America's world role harbored "a strong antipathy toward entangling alliances, a large peacetime military establishment, and the centralization of authority in the national government" and they argued that the "rise of the national security state necessarily entailed economic and political adaptations that could undermine the very traditions and institutions that had made America great." This view was opposed by a new cultural discourse—extolling the virtues of the "national security state"—that blossomed as the Cold War intensified. As Hogan notes, the advocates of the national security state "borrowed from a cultural narrative that celebrated American exceptionalism and American destiny" and argued that "leadership of the free world was a scared mission thrust upon the American people by divine Providence, and the laws of both history and nature." The Bush II administration has used 9/11 to breathe new life into this outlook, which forms the bedrock of the case for American primacy and empire. At the same time, the morass of Iraq, the economic costs of empire, and the Bush II administration's assault on civil liberties—exemplified by the Patriot Act and revelations of National Security Agency eavesdropping—have given a new resonance to the deepest fear held by those who have favored a foreign policy of restraint: that in the course of attempting to transform the world, the United States would succeed only in transforming itself.

Overview of the Chapter

In this chapter, I argue that primacy and empire is a strategy that will lead to bad consequences for the United States. Rather than bringing the United States peace and security, the pursuit of primacy and empire will result in a geopolitical backlash against the United States. It already has. The 9/11 attacks were a violent reaction against America's primacy—and specifically against its imperial ambitions in the Middle East. Similarly, the quagmire in Iraq also is a direct consequence of U.S. imperial aspirations. And it will not end there. Because it is premised on the belief that the United States must embark on assertive policies to bring about regime change by imposing democracy abroad, the pursuit of primacy and empire will drag the United States into otherwise avoidable wars—what one proponent of the strategy has termed "savage wars for peace." Looking ahead, if the United States continues to follow its current strategy of primacy and empire, it almost certainly will find itself on a collision course with Iran (and possibly North Korea and Syria) and—more importantly—China.

In this chapter, I argue that primacy and empire are the cause of American *in*security. The balance of this chapter unfolds as follows. First, I place the debate about primacy and empire in historical context and examine the intellectual foundations of current American strategy. Second, I show why the pursuit of primacy is a counterproductive—even dangerous—strategy for the United States. Third, I examine the imperial dimension of American strategy, especially the push for regime change and democratic transformation abroad. Here, I focus on the Iraq war, because this reckless adventure was all but mandated by the logic of the strategy of primacy and empire.

Before and after 9/11: The Historical Backdrop to the Strategy of Primacy and Empire

9/11: What Did Not Change

It is often said that 9/11 "changed everything" with respect to U.S. foreign policy. In the most fundamental sense, however, this is not true. From 1991 to 9/11, the key debate about the United States' role in the world was about American primacy. This remained true after 9/11. The United States, of course, was catapulted into a position of primacy when its superpower rival, the Soviet Union, collapsed between 1989 and 1991. That is, when the Cold War ended the United States was left standing (as U.S. policy-makers liked to put it) as the "sole remaining superpower" in the international system. With no actual or potential geopolitical—or ideological—rivals in sight, America enjoyed an historically unprecedented dominance in international politics. At the same time, the fact that the United States attained primacy as result of the Soviet Union's downfall should not obscure the fact that from the early 1940s onwards, gaining geopolitical primacy was the overriding objective of U.S. grand strategy.[6]

American primacy has two distinct meanings. On the one hand, primacy describes an objective *fact* of international politics. The United States today is—as it has been for some fifteen years—far and away the most powerful state in the international system. On the other hand, primacy is also a *policy*, because since the Cold War's end America's paramount grand strategic goal has been to maintain a firm grip on its preeminent international role. Although there has been widespread agreement among foreign policy analysts favoring the strategy of primacy, neoconservative foreign policy intellectuals have been its most articulate proponents. The writings of William Kristol and Robert Kagan are illustrative. They argued that, having prevailed in the Cold War, "The United States enjoys strategic and ideological predominance. The first objective of U.S. foreign policy should be to preserve and enhance that predominance by strengthening America's security, supporting its friends, advancing its interests, and standing up for its principles around the world."[7] For them, in the Cold War's aftermath, "the appropriate goal of American foreign policy is to preserve [U.S.] hegemony as far into the future as possible."[8] The proponents of primacy and empire like a "unipolar" world—as long as the United States is on top—and want to keep it that way. As one neoconservative intellectual puts it: "A unipolar world is fine, if America is the uni."[9]

The flip side of this belief that a unipolar world dominated by the United States is the best of all possible worlds is the corresponding belief that a multipolar world—that is, an international system composed of three or more great powers—is the worst of all possible worlds. According to neoconservative pundit Charles Krauthammer, multipolarity is not only "inherently fluid and unpredictable," but also "unstable and bloody."[10] The way to prevent multipolar instability, it has been claimed, is to maintain U.S. primacy. As Kristol and Kagan put it, "American hegemony is the only reliable defense of peace and international order."[11] Similarly, Zalmay Khalilzad—a senior Pentagon official in the Bush I administration, who has served as ambassador both to Afghanistan and Iraq during the Bush II administration—argued that "U.S. leadership [i.e., continued American primacy] would be more conducive to global stability than a bipolar or a multipolar balance of power system."[12] Consequently, it was said, to preserve its primacy and avoid a reversion to multipolarity, the United States should use its hard power to prevent the emergence of new great powers ("peer competitors"). As Kagan and Kristol put it, "In Europe, in Asia, and the Middle East, the message we should be sending to potential foes is: 'Don't even think about it.'"[13] The primacist vision of American grand strategy has been adopted by all three post–Cold War administrations.

The official U.S. position on the prospect of a post–Cold War multipolar system was set forth clearly in the *Regional Defense Strategy*, which was prepared by the Pentagon during the Bush I administration: "It is not in our interest...to return to earlier periods in which multiple military powers balanced one against another in what passed for security structures, while regional, or even global peace hung in the balance."[14] This stance was reiterated during the Bush II administration by Condoleezza Rice, who found it "troubling" that "some have spoken admiringly—even nostalgically—of 'multipolarity,' as if it were a good thing, to be desired for its own sake." She made it clear that from Washington's standpoint, multipolarity is not a good thing at all.[15] U.S. hostility to multipolarity was underscored in the Bush II administration's *2002 National Security Strategy*, which declared that the United States is "attentive to the possible renewal of old patterns of great power competition."[16] For the Bush I, Clinton, and Bush II administrations, the antidote to multipolar "instability" has been U.S. primacy.

This first was made clear during the Bush I administration. The administration's draft *Defense Planning Guidance* (*DPG*) for fiscal years 1994–1999—which was written under the supervision of the neoconservative Paul Wolfowitz, then serving as a senior Pentagon official—was leaked to the *New York Times*.[17] The *DPG* made clear that the objective of U.S. grand strategy henceforth would be to maintain America's preponderance by preventing the emergence of new great power rivals, stating that "we must maintain the mechanisms for *deterring potential competitors from even aspiring to a larger regional or global role*."[18] The Clinton administration embraced the strategy of primacy, as has the Bush II administration, which, in its 2002 *National Security Strategy* declared that the aim of U.S. strategy is to prevent a would-be peer competitor from "surpassing, or *even equaling* the power of the United States."[19]

9/11: What Did Change

The strategy of primacy was in place well before 9/11, and it remains so. In this respect, U.S. policy was not changed by 9/11. But 9/11 did change American grand strategy in one important respect: it gave rise to voices calling for the muscular assertion of U.S. power to create a new American Empire. Yet, in saying this, care must be exercised. Although the question of whether the United States *should* be an empire has been contested at least since the Spanish–American War (1898), it is undeniable that America *has* been an empire for a long time. Similarly, although the proponents of a new American Empire have called for regime change and the promotion of democracy abroad, this too is hardly a new departure in U.S. foreign policy. These have been key features of American policy since Woodrow Wilson's time. More recently, the "enlargement" of democracy was the centerpiece of the Clinton administration's grand strategy. Moreover, President Bill Clinton himself, as well as other key administration officials, made it clear that the United States had the right to intervene in the domestic affairs of nondemocratic states. As President Clinton declared in April 1993:

> During the Cold War our foreign policies largely focused on relations among nations. Our strategies sought a balance of power to keep the peace. *Today, our policies must also focus on relations within nations, on a nation's form of governance, on its economic structure, on its ethnic tolerance. These are of concern to us, for they shape how these nations treat their neighbors as well as their own people and whether they are reliable when they give their word.*[20]

And, well before President George W. Bush proclaimed that America's democratic values are "universal," President Clinton said the same thing—specifically, that those values are a "universal aspiration."[21]

Notwithstanding these continuities in U.S. policy, 9/11 *did* change some things. First, it brought about a dramatic change in the tone of the Bush II administration's foreign policy. It is easy to forget that during the 2000 presidential campaign, candidate George W. Bush intimated that he understood that the strategy of primacy could boomerang against the United States. He said that, if elected, under his administration the United States would be guided by "realism," act on the world stage with "humility," renounce the Wilsonian idealism of the Clinton administration (and, although he, of course, did not say so, also of the Bush I administration), and forego "nation-building" abroad. After 9/11, of course, the Bush II administration embraced both the substance and the rhetoric of primacy and empire—indeed, compared to the Bush I and Clinton administrations, the Bush II administration approach was primacy and empire on stimulants.

The jarring contrast between George W. Bush's foreign policy stance during the 2000 election and its post-9/11 rhetoric and policies raises an interesting question: Did Bush's statements as a candidate sincerely reflect his foreign policy preferences? Put another way, but for 9/11 would the Bush II administration have renounced the strategy of primacy? Almost certainly not. The Bush II administration brought to power a number of policy-makers who either were "neoconservatives" or were strongly influenced in their foreign policy views by the arguments that have been advanced beginning in the 1990s by neoconservative intellectuals, including *Weekly Standard* editor William Kristol, Robert Kagan, Max Boot, Charles Krauthammer, Ben Wattenberg, and the British historian (and now Harvard professor) Niall Ferguson. Foremost among these administration officials were Vice President Dick Cheney, Defense Secretary Donald Rumsfeld, senior Defense Department officials Paul Wolfowitz and Douglas Feith, Richard Perle, presidential speechwriter David Frum, and Cheney's former national security adviser, I. Lewis ("Scooter") Libby.

These officials came to office with an expansive view of America's interests in the world. As James Mann has observed, their "vision was that of an unchallengeable America, a United States whose military power was so awesome that it no longer needed to make compromises or accommodations (unless it chose to do so) with any other nation or groups of countries."[22] Indeed, even before 9/11 there were signs—its hard-line stance with respect to China and North Korea, its decision to build a national missile defense system despite the qualms of the NATO allies, and its skepticism toward international treaties—that the administration would prefer primacy to "humility." For the administration's primacists, 9/11 was an almost providential event that gave them a green light to follow the policy course—a highly militarized and confrontational strategy of primacy—that they would have wished to pursue in any event, but for which they might otherwise have lacked public and congressional support—especially applying the strategy of empire to gain dominance in the Middle East.

It is here, perhaps, that the events of 9/11 most obviously changed American grand strategy. 9/11 accelerated the morphing of the post–Cold War debate about American *primacy* into a debate about American *empire*. Of course, although the notion of an American Empire is nothing new, most Americans undoubtedly believe that the United States is not—and never has been—an empire. After all, one of the first history lessons Americans learn is that the United States gained independence by rebelling against Britain's imperial rule. And, at least since Woodrow Wilson's time, the United States has presented itself to the world as an opponent of (European) imperialism and a champion of anticolonialism. And, of course, U.S. policy-makers routinely deny that America harbors imperial ambitions. As President George W. Bush declared in his January 2004 State of the Union address, "We have no desire to dominate, no ambitions of empire."[23] These denials resonate with Americans, who tend to think that empire involves land-grabbing and flag-planting in overseas territories.

The truth, however, is different. From its inception, the United States has been a nation driven by imperial ambitions and a corresponding sense of national mission. As Richard Van Alstyne has noted, the Founding Fathers believed that the United States was a "rising empire"; that is, a nation "that would expand in population and territory, and increase in strength and territory."[24] Until the War Between the States, America's territorial expansion was confined to the North American continent and did not take place overseas, which may explain why Americans tend not to think of this period of U.S. history as an age of American imperialism. This expansion was both ruthless and aggressive and came at the expense of the European great powers that had North American interests (Britain, France, Spain), of Mexico (in the war of conquest initiated by the United States in 1846), and, of course, the native American Indians who had the misfortune to find themselves in the way as the United States fulfilled its "Manifest Destiny" by expanding all the way to the Pacific Ocean from its original enclave on the Atlantic seaboard.

For sure, it is commonplace to believe that empires are based on the conquest and direct rule of overseas lands—literally planting the flag on foreign soil. Following the Spanish–American War, of course, the United States did flirt briefly with this traditional form of imperialism, when it acquired the Philippines and Puerto Rico, and (at about the same time) annexed Hawaii. However, for the modern American Empire, the acquisition of colonies has been the exception, not the rule. This kind of formal imperialism is not the only way a powerful state can establish an empire abroad. A great power also can establish an *informal* empire by using its military and economic muscle—and its culture and ideology (what foreign policy analysts frequently call "soft power")—to install and maintain compliant, friendly regimes in foreign territories. By ruling indirectly through local elites, an imperial power can forego the burdens of direct colonial rule. The American Empire since 1900 has followed this path. Specifically, American imperialism has taken the form of what Ronald Robinson and John Gallagher described as the "imperialism of free trade" and what William Appleman Williams called the "imperialism of idealism"—that is, by democracy promotion and regime change.

The new—post–Cold War and post-9/11—American Empire traces its lineage directly to the old American Empire of the twentieth century, the geographic core of which was western Europe and East Asia. But 9/11 did mark a change in the way policy-makers conceive of the American Empire. The new American Empire is distinguished from the old American Empire by its geographical focal point—the Middle East—and by its breathtaking ambition of transforming the Islamic world. As the invasion of Iraq demonstrated, it is an empire constructed on the marriage of raw military power and a militant ideology. In the early 1990s, neoconservative foreign policy thinkers began developing the concepts that would provide the intellectual framework for the new American Empire. First, the United States would have to deal with dangerous "rogue states" and ensure they did not acquire nuclear, chemical, or biological weapons (the so-called weapons of mass destruction; WMD). These rogue states invariably did not share America's democratic values, which, as the neoconservative architects of the American Empire viewed it, is precisely what made them rogue states. Thus, second, the United States had both the right, and the obligation, to use its power "to shape the international environment to its own advantage" by "actively promoting American principles and governance abroad—democracy, free markets, respect for liberty."[25] The architects of the current American Empire made clear that U.S. strategy would seek to promote America's interests *and* its values. Indeed, for them the two were identical, because as the neoconservative foreign policy intellectuals saw it, to be secure the United States would have to export liberal democratic principles. Well before the Bush II administration spoke of the "axis of evil," or "outposts of tyranny," neoconservative foreign policy thinkers had pinpointed exactly which states were in their geopolitical crosshairs *and* what the United States should do about them: "in the post–Cold War era a principal aim of American foreign policy should be to bring about a change of regime in hostile nations—in Baghdad and Belgrade, in Pyongyang and Beijing, and wherever tyrannical governments acquire the military power to threaten their neighbors, their allies, or the United States itself."[26]

The foundations of America's post-9/11 imperial Middle Eastern policy were in place well before the events of 9/11. In January 1998, for example, many of the neoconservative architects of the current American Empire wrote an open letter to President Bill Clinton arguing that "removing Saddam Hussein and his regime from power...now needs to become the aim of American foreign policy."[27] Neoconservatives had a long track record of virulent, ideologically tinged hostility to Islamic fundamentalism. After 9/11, their views came to the forefront of the U.S. foreign policy debate. Foreshadowing the Bush II administration's crusade against "Islamofascism," in November 2001 Charles Krauthammer depicted the threat posed by *al Qaeda* as similar to that posed by Nazi Germany and the Soviet Union: "We have an enemy, radical Islam; it is a global opponent of worldwide reach, armed with an idea, and with the tactics, weapons, and ruthlessness necessary to take on the world's hegemon; and its defeat is our supreme national objective, as overriding a necessity as were the defeats of fascism and Soviet communism."[28] 9/11, it was said, demonstrated that the United States was involved in "a new existential struggle, this time with an enemy even more fanatical, fatalistic and indeed undeterrable than in the past."[29]

9/11 enabled the neoconservatives to translate their transformational, imperial aspirations for the Middle East into actual U.S. policy. As James Mann has pointed out, even before 9/11, the architects of the new American Empire had concluded that with the Cold War's end, the United States no longer needed to tie its regional policies to authoritarian regimes like Saudi Arabia and those of the Gulf emirates.[30] The region was, they believed, ripe for a democratic transformation. That, or so they say, is the only way to "get to the root of the problem, which is the cauldron of political oppression, religious intolerance and social ruin in the Arab-Islamic world—oppression transmuted and deflected by regimes with no legitimacy into the virulent, murderous anti-Americanism that exploded upon us on 9/11."[31] 9/11 was both the catalyst, and the pretext, for the United States to put this policy into effect. Whether the United States could have pursued these ambitions of causing a democratic transformation in the Middle East prior to 9/11 is doubtful, but 9/11 opened the door for the Bush II administration to attempt to incorporate the Middle East into the American Empire.

The Case against the American Empire

Preserving American Hegemony

American hegemony today is an objective fact, reflecting the absence of other great powers (what U.S. strategists call "peer competitors") and U.S. hard power. The Soviet Union's collapse, of course, removed from the geopolitical equation the one state capable of acting as a counterweight to American power. No other state has stepped up to fill this geopolitical vacuum created by its downfall. Indeed, the sheer magnitude of U.S. power makes it difficult—and possibly dangerous—for other states to emerge as countervailing power centers. Militarily, American power is awesome. The United States spends more on defense than the rest of the world combined. And U.S. superiority is qualitative, not just quantitative. Presently, no state can compare with the U.S. military skills in high-tech conventional warfare. The United States enjoys a commanding advantage in the use of stealth aircraft, precision-guided munitions, the integrated use of computer systems and reconnaissance and communications satellites, and long-range power projection capabilities. Moreover, the United States enjoys a commanding advantage in nuclear weapons. Indeed, the United States has a first-strike capability against China and may have a similar advantage over Russia. Economically, the story is the same.

The U.S. economy remains far and away the largest economy in the world (far ahead of number two Japan, and even farther ahead of fast-rising China).

Given this formidable—indeed, overwhelming—hard power, the obvious question is what is wrong with a strategy that seeks to preserve American primacy; that is, U.S. dominance of a unipolar world? After all, the strategy does have both an intuitive, and a logical, plausibility. Power *is* important in international politics, and the United States today has a lot of it. What could be better than being the only great power in a unipolar world? The obvious answer (the answer given by advocates of primacy) is "nothing could be better," and, hence, the United States should do everything it can to perpetuate its current geopolitical preeminence. Indeed, if the Duchess of Windsor had been an American strategist she doubtless would have said that the United States can never be too rich, too powerful, or too well armed. In the abstract, it is difficult to quarrel with this line of thinking. In the real world, however, the attempt to preserve American primacy is likely to backfire against the United States.

The Fate of Hegemons: Why Other States Will "Balance" against American Primacy

The intellectual foundation for American primacy is what is known as "offensive realist" theory.[32] This is one of several versions of the realist approach to international politics. Offensive realism holds that the best strategy for a great power is to gain primacy because, if it can do so, it will not face any serious challenges to its security. There are two reasons why offensive realists believe this to be true. First, if a great power successfully gains primacy, its overwhelming power will dissuade others from challenging it. Second, primacy alleviates uncertainty about other states' intentions and about the present and future distribution of power in the international system. As John Mearshimer puts it, in the dog-eat-dog world of great power politics, "states quickly understand that the best way to ensure their survival is to be the most powerful state in the system."[33] Simply put, the grand strategy prescribed by offensive realism is that a great power should grab all the power it can get. This certainly is what the United States has sought to do since the Cold War's end.

At first glance, the logic of offensive realism appears to be compelling. However, when looked at closely, it leaves out some factors that have—or should have—a crucial role in grand strategic calculations. The most important of these is geography. Offensive realist theory is based on the history of multipolar European great power politics that ended only in 1945. On the Continent, multiple great powers contended for supremacy in a geographically compact area. Geopolitically speaking, Europe was a tough neighborhood where each of the major powers was always at risk of being attacked, and conquered, by its nearby rivals. Under these conditions, gaining primacy—what historian A.J.P. Taylor called "the mastery of Europe"—was the only way to break out of the permanent state of insecurity and fear that characterized Continental power politics.

However, while offensive realism explains the behavior of Continental powers, it does a poor job of accounting for the grand strategies of offshore—or insular—great powers like Great Britain (during its imperial heyday) or—even more so—the United States since 1900. Britain and the United States have been shielded both by geography and their own considerable military capabilities from invasion. Indeed, the United States has been—and is—the most secure great power in history. The reasons are well known. The United States has been blessed with weak neighbors on the North American continent and has been protected from hostile rivals by the vast expanse of the Atlantic and Pacific Oceans. The defensive impact of geography has been reinforced by U.S. naval and air power, and, after, 1945, by its nuclear deterrent capabilities. Even after 9/11, the United States is all but invulnerable to *existential* threats emanating from abroad. To put it another way, the logic of offensive realism does not apply to the United States: the United States does *not* need to seek global primacy to gain security because it *already* is secure. Moreover, there is a compelling reason for the United States to forego the goal of maintaining its global primacy.

Counterpoised against offensive realism is another variant of realist theory: balance of power realism. Balance of power theorists argue that in one way, at least, international politics is like physics: every action triggers a reaction. Specifically, when one great power becomes too powerful—that is, verges on, or gains, primacy—other great powers respond by "balancing" against it. That is, they build up their military capabilities (internal balancing) and/or enter into alliances with other great powers (external balancing) to stop it. The reason is simple: when one state becomes too powerful, it threatens other states' security.

States are ever-vigilant when it comes to maintaining their security because they want to survive as independent players in international politics. Up to a point, therefore, it is a good thing for a state to be powerful. But when a state becomes *too* powerful, it frightens others; in self-defense, they seek to offset and contain those great powers that aspire to primacy. And the ironclad lesson of history is clear: states that bid for hegemony (primacy) invariably fail. As Henry A. Kissinger has said, "hegemonic empires almost automatically elicit universal resistance, which is why all such claimants have sooner or later exhausted themselves."[34] Indeed, the history of modern international politics is strewn with the geopolitical wreckage of states that bid unsuccesfully for primacy: The Hapsburg Empire under Charles V, France under Louis XIV and Napoleon, Victorian Britain, Germany under Hitler. By pursuing a strategy of primacy, the United States today risks the same fate that has befallen other great powers that have striven to dominate the international political system.

Is American Primacy Different?

Despite the impressive historical evidence that the quest for primacy ends in ruin, the proponents of American primacy claim that the United States is an exception to the rule. Here, two arguments are commonly invoked. One is the assertion that the United States' lead in hard power is so massive that no other state(s) can even aspire to catch up with the United States.[35] The second claim is somewhat different: even if other states could emerge as peer competitors to the United States, they have no incentive actually to do so because they do not perceive *American* primacy as threatening. On the contrary, U.S. primacy is unique—or so it is said—because the United States is a "benevolent" hegemon. Both of these assertions contain just enough truth to be superficially plausible. However, when examined a bit more closely, neither of them provides an accurate gauge of the future of American primacy.

Can the United States Be Caught?   Up to a point, the primacists are correct. In terms of hard power, there *is* a yawning gap between the United States and the next-ranking powers. It will take some time before any other state emerges as a true "peer competitor" of the United States. Nevertheless, at some point within the next decade or two, new great power rivals to the United States will emerge. To put it slightly differently, American primacy cannot be sustained indefinitely. The relative power position of great powers is dynamic, not static, which means that at any point in time some states are gaining in relative power while others are losing it. Thus, as Paul Kennedy has observed, no great power ever has been able "to remain *permanently* ahead of all others, because that would imply a freezing of the differentiated pattern of growth rates, technological advance, and military developments which has existed since time immemorial."[36] Even the most ardent primacists know this to be true, which is why they concede that American primacy won't last forever. Indeed, the leading primacists acknowledge, that—*at best*—the United States will not be able to hold onto its primacy much beyond 2030. There are indications, however, that American primacy could end much sooner than that. Already there is evidence suggesting that new great powers are in the process of emerging. This is what the current debate in the United States about the implications of China's rise is all about. But China isn't the only factor in play, and transition from U.S. primacy to multipolarity may be much closer than primacists want to admit. For example, in its survey of likely international developments up until 2020, the CIA's National Intelligence Council's report *Mapping the Global Future* notes:

> The likely emergence of China and India as new major global players—similar to the rise of Germany in the 19th century and the United States in the early 20th century—will transform the geopolitical landscape, with impacts potentially as dramatic as those of the previous two

centuries. In the same way that commentators refer to the 1900s as the American Century, the early 21st century may be seen as the time when some in the developing world led by China and India came into their own.[37]

In a similar vein, a recent study by the CIA's Strategic Assessment Group projects that by 2020 both China (which *Mapping the Global Future* pegs as "by any measure a first-rate military power" around 2020) and the European Union will come close to matching the United States in terms of their respective shares of world power.[38] For sure, there are always potential pitfalls in projecting current trends several decades into the future (not least is that it is not easy to convert economic power into effective military power). But if the ongoing shift in the distribution of relative power continues, new poles of power in the international system are likely to emerge during the next decade or two. The real issue is not *if* American primacy will end, but *how soon* it will end.

Is America a Benevolent Hegemon?   The second leg of the argument that U.S. primacy is an exception to the rule rests on three closely related claims. First, other states—at least those that are not rogue states, "outposts of tyranny," or part of the "axis of evil"—will not resist American primacy because U.S. power does not threaten them. Second, many other states do not fear American power because they share liberal democratic values with the United States. Third, others' fears of U.S. power are assuaged because the United States acts altruistically and does good things for the international system. Indeed, because other states benefit in many ways from American primacy, they supposedly regard the United States not as a threat, but as a positive factor in international politics. As Michael Mandelbaum puts it, the United States may be Goliath in international politics, "but it is a benign one."[39] He goes on to argue:

> The United States does not endanger other countries, nor does it invariably act without regard to the interests and wishes of others. Second, far from menacing the world, the United States plays a uniquely positive global role. The governments of most other countries understand that, although they have powerful reasons not to say so explicitly.[40]

This argument cannot simply be dismissed out of hand.

American primacy *does* benefit the world in some ways. Scholars of international political economy have devised an explanation—"hegemonic stability theory"—to show just why this is so. Like Britain during the period from 1814 to 1914, American military and economic power provides the framework for an open, economically interdependent—in today's catchword, "globalized"—international economy. The U.S. dollar is the international economy's "reserve currency," which serves as the medium of exchange and thus lubricates international trade and investment. Through the huge outflow of dollars—a combined effect of the U.S. merchandise trade deficit, overseas investments by American firms, and foreign aid and military expenditures overseas—the United States provides the international economy with liquidity. The United States—generally acting through institutions that it controls like the International Monetary Fund (IMF)—also is the international economy's "lender of last resort." American largess—typically in the form of low-interest loans by the IMF—is what keeps tottering economies in East Asia, Mexico, and Latin America from going belly-up. Finally, the United States is the world's market, or consumer, of last resort. Americans' seemingly insatiable demand for overseas products—cars, electronics, computers, apparel—drives the growth of overseas economies like those of China, India, South Korea, and Latin America. The boundless appetite of U.S. consumers for foreign goods is the locomotive force for global economic growth.

Other countries also benefit from American military power. Wars are bad for business, and the U.S. military presence abroad supposedly "reassures" East Asia and Europe that these regions will remain stable and peaceful, thereby contributing to economic confidence. As Defense Secretary Donald Rumsfeld put it, other states "think of the value [U.S.-provided] security provides the world, and the fact that all of the economic activity that takes place is stunted and frightened by instability and fear...."[41] Moreover, the U.S. military protects the "global commons" of air, sea, and space—the avenues through which information is transmitted, and through which goods and people flow from nation to nation. Most important, because many states abroad live in dangerous neighborhoods, the forward deployment of U.S. military forces protects them from troublemakers that live nearby. Moreover, because American military power supposedly is "off-shore," the United States does not threaten the security of other states. As Stephen Walt puts it, "The United States is by far the world's most *powerful* state, but it does not pose a significant *threat* to the vital interests of the major powers."[42]

According to primacists, far from being apprehensive about American hard power and balancing against the United States, other states eagerly seek to shelter under the protective umbrella that American primacy provides. Consequently, in Europe, the United States ensures Russia and east central Europe that they will not be menaced by resurgent Germany while simultaneously protecting east central Europe from a revived Russian threat. In East Asia, the situation is similar. There, American military power shields Japan and Taiwan from China, and South Korea from North Korea. In the Middle East, the U.S. military commitment protects Saudi Arabia and the oil-producing Gulf emirates—and Israel—from Iran (just as it protected them before March 2003 from Saddam Hussein's Iraq). According to the proponents of the American primacy, by maintaining order in these regions, the United States keeps a lid on long-simmering historical animosities, precludes national rivalries from resurfacing and forestalls destabilizing arms races—and possibly major war.

A final reason that others supposedly regard American primacy as "benevolent" is because the United States is a *liberal* hegemon. As such, it is said, America's "soft power"—its ideals, political institutions, and culture—draws other states into Washington's orbit. As Harvard professor Joseph S. Nye Jr., asserts, because of America's soft power "others do not see us as a threat, but rather as an attraction."[43] In a similar vein, G. John Ikenberry and Charles Kupchan have argued that the liberal democratic nature of America's domestic political system legitimates U.S. primacy and simultaneously reassures others that the United States will exercise its power with restraint.[44] As one neoconservative commentator has put it, the rest of the world accepts American primacy because they "know that they have little to fear or distrust from a righteous state."[45] This belief routinely is echoed in official pronouncements, such as a Pentagon policy statement that declared: "Our fundamental belief in democracy and human rights gives other nations confidence that our significant military power threatens no one's aspirations for peaceful democratic progress."[46] All in all, the liberal nature of American primacy supposedly reinforces the confidence of other states that—its vast power notwithstanding—the United States is not a threat because, as G. John Ikenberry puts it, it "is a mature, *status quo* power that pursues a restrained and accommodating grand strategy."[47]

The truth, however, is that the United States is not at all a status quo power. Now, for sure, the American primacists are content with the prevailing unipolar status quo. That is, they want the make sure that the United States retains its role as the sole superpower. But in a more fundamental sense, the United States is the antithesis of a status quo power. Rather, it is an expansionist power that constantly is attempting to add to its lead in relative power vis-à-vis potential rivals; extend the territorial reach of its military power (for example, by acquiring new bases in Central Asia); and enlarge its influence ideologically by spreading "democracy" worldwide. Indeed, the whole debate about the new American Empire underscores the expansionist impulses driving U.S. grand strategy today. If any doubt existed on this point, the American invasion of Iraq in March 2003 dispelled it. Around the world, Iraq removed the veil of American "benevolence" and revealed to the rest of the world the aggrandizing and self-interested nature of U.S. grand strategy.

The claim that others regard American primacy as benevolent because of U.S. *soft* power and shared values is similarly dubious. And again, Iraq played an important role in exploding this myth. Beginning with the run-up to the invasion of Iraq to the present, one public opinion survey after another has revealed that a vast "values gap" exists between the United States and the rest of the world. Tellingly, this gap exists not just between the United States and East Asia and the Middle East, but between the United States and Europe. One would think that if there is any part of the world where shared values really do cause others to view American primacy as benevolent, Europe would be the place. Yet, a September 2004 poll of eight thousand respondents on both sides of the Atlantic found that 83 percent of Americans, and 79 percent of Europeans, agreed that Europe and the United States have different social and cultural values.[48] On a host of issues—including the death penalty, the role of religion in everyday life, and attitudes toward the role of international law and institutions—Europeans and Americans hold divergent views, not common ones. The Iraq war has exposed the huge gulf in values that gradually is causing the United States and Europe to drift apart—in large measure because Europe regards the United States as being a geopolitical rogue elephant, rather than as a "benevolent hegemon." The problem with rogue elephants, of course, is that when they are on the loose anyone nearby is at risk of being trampled. This is why other states are uneasy about American primacy.

For sure, many states do benefit both economically and in terms of security from American primacy. And it also is true that not *all* other states will feel threatened by U.S. hard power. Eventually, however, some of the other states in the international political system *are* going to believe that they are menaced by American primacy. For example, far from being "off-shore" as the primacists claim, U.S. power is very much on shore—or lurking just beyond the coastline—and very much in the faces of China, Russia, and the Islamic world. And, in this sense, international politics is not a lot different than basketball: players who push others around and get in their faces are likely to be the targets of a self-defensive punch in the nose.

Doubtless, American primacy has its dimension of benevolence, but a state as powerful as the United States can never be benevolent *enough* to offset the fear that other states have of its unchecked power. In international politics, benevolent hegemons are like unicorns—there is no such animal. Hegemons love themselves, but others mistrust and fear them—and for good reason. In today's world, others dread both the overconcentration of geopolitical weight in America's favor and the purposes for which it may be used. After all, "No great power has a monopoly on virtue and, although some may have a great deal more virtue than others, virtue imposed on others is not seen as such by them. All great powers are capable of exercising a measure of self-restraint, but they are tempted not to and the choice to practice restraint is made easier by the existence of countervailing power and the possibility of it being exercised."[49] While Washington's self-proclaimed benevolence is inherently ephemeral, the hard fist of American power is tangible. Others must worry constantly that if U.S. intentions change, bad things may happen to them. In a one-superpower world, the overconcentration of power in America's hands is an omnipresent challenge to other states' security, and Washington's ability to reassure others of its benevolence is limited by the very enormity of its power.

American Hegemony: 9/11 and Beyond

Contrary to what its proponents claim, in at least three respects, primacy causes *in*security for the United States. First, even before 9/11 and the invasion of Iraq, the heavy hand of U.S. primacy pressed down on the Middle East, as the United States sought to establish political, military, and cultural ascendancy in the region. Terrorist groups like *al Qaeda* are a form of blowback against long-standing U.S. policies in the Middle East and the Persian Gulf—including American support for authoritarian regimes in the region, and uncritical support for Israel in its conflict with the Palestinians. America's current strategy of primacy and empire also means that the United States is on a collision course with China and Iran. In both cases, the logic of U.S. strategy suggests that preventive and preemptive options are on the table to thwart the rise of a prospective peer competitor (China) and a regional rival (Iran). Tensions with China and Iran also are being fueled by the liberal—Wilsonian— thrust of American strategy that challenges the legitimacy of nondemocratic regimes while aggressively aiming at the promotion of democracy abroad.

Terrorism: When Over There Becomes Over Here   9/11 was not a random act of violence visited upon the United States. The United States was the target of *al Qaeda's* terrorist strikes because that group harbored specific political grievances against the United States. If we step back for a moment from our horror and revulsion at the events of September 11, we can see that the attack was in keeping with the Clausewitzian paradigm of war: force was used against the United States by its adversaries to advance their political objectives. As Michael Scheurer, who headed the CIA analytical team monitoring Osama bin Laden and *al Qaeda*, put it, "In the context of ideas bin Laden shares with his brethren, the military actions of al Qaeda and its allies are acts of war, not terrorism...meant to advance bin Laden's clear, focused, limited, and widely popular foreign policy goals...."[50] Terrorism, Bruce Hoffman says, is "about power: the pursuit of power, the acquisition of power, and use of power to achieve political change."[51] As Clausewitz himself observed, "war is not an act of senseless passion but is controlled by its political object."[52] Terrorism really is a form of asymmetric warfare waged against the United States by groups that lack the military wherewithal to slug it out with the United States toe-to-toe. 9/11 was a violent counterreaction to America's geopolitical—and cultural—primacy. As Richard K. Betts presciently observed in a 1998 *Foreign Affairs* article, "It is hardly likely that Middle Eastern radicals would be hatching schemes like the destruction of the World Trade Center if the United States had not been identified so long as the mainstay of Israel, the shah of Iran, and conservative Arab regimes and the source of a cultural assault on Islam."[53] U.S. primacy fuels terrorist groups like *al Qaeda* and fans Islamic fundamentalism, which is a form of "blowback" against America's preponderance and its world role.[54] As long as the United States uses its global primacy to impose its imperial sway on regions like the Persian Gulf, it will be the target of politically motivated terrorist groups like *al Qaeda*.

After 9/11, many foreign policy analysts and pundits asked the question, "Why do they hate us?" This question missed the key point, however. No doubt, there are Islamic fundamentalists who do "hate" the United States for cultural, religious, and ideological reasons. And, for sure, notwithstanding American neoconservatives' obvious relish for making it so, to some extent the War on Terrorism inescapably has overtones of a "clash of civilizations." Still, this isn't—and should not be allowed to become—a replay of the Crusades. As Scheuer says, "one of the greatest dangers for Americans in deciding how to confront the Islamist threat lies in continuing to believe—at the urging of senior U.S. leaders—that Muslims hate and attack us for what we are and think, rather than for what we do."[55] The United States may be greatly reviled in some quarters of the Islamic world, but were the United States not so intimately involved in the affairs of the Middle East, it's hardly likely that this detestation would have manifested itself as violently as it did on 9/11.

Experts on terrorism understand the political motives that drive the actions of groups like *al Qaeda*. In his important recent study of suicide terrorists, Robert A. Pape found that what "nearly all suicide terrorist attacks have in common is a specific secular and strategic goal: to compel modern democracies to withdraw military forces from territory that the terrorists consider to be their homeland."[56] Pape found that "even *al Qaeda* fits this pattern: although Saudi Arabia is not under American military occupation *per se*, a principal objective of Osama bin Laden is the expulsion of American troops from the Persian Gulf and the reduction of Washington's power in the region."[57] This finding is seconded by Scheuer, who describes bin Laden's objectives as: "the end of U.S. aid to Israel and the ultimate elimination of that state; the removal of U.S. and Western forces from the Arabian Peninsula; the removal of U.S. and Western military forces from Iraq, Afghanistan, and other Muslim lands; the end of U.S. support for oppression of Muslims by Russia, China, and India; the end of U.S. protection for repressive, apostate Muslim regimes in Saudi Arabia, Kuwait, Egypt, Jordan, et cetera; and the conservation of the Muslim world's energy resources and their sale at higher prices."[58] Simply put, it is American primacy, and the *policies* that flow from it, that have made the United States a lightning rod for Islamic anger.

The Coming Clash with China   Almost from the moment the Soviet Union collapsed, American officials have worried about the strategic implications of China's rise. U.S. policy toward China during the last three administrations has been complex. All three post–Cold War administrations have made clear that they are not prepared to countenance China's emergence as a peer competitor. The United States, however, is willing to give China the opportunity to integrate itself into the American-led international order—on Washington's terms. Thus, the United States encourages China to become a "responsible member of the international community."[59] "Responsibility," however, is defined as Beijing's willingness to accept Washington's vision of a stable international order.[60] Specifically, "responsibility" means that Beijing "adjusts to the international rules developed over the last century"; in particular, to the international security and economic frameworks that were created following World War II by a dominant United States.[61] "Responsibility," as President Bush reiterated in his November 2005 speech in Kyoto, also means China's domestic political liberalization and its development as a free market economy firmly anchored to the international economy.[62] As the Bush II administration's 2002 *National Security Strategy* declares, "America will encourage the advancement of democracy and economic openness" in China "because these are the best foundations for domestic stability and international order." As Deputy Secretary of State Robert B. Zoellick underscored, "closed politics cannot be a permanent feature of Chinese society."[63] If anything, the Bush II administration's 2006 *National Security Strategy* suggests that the United States' insistence on China's democratization has hardened. As that document states:

> The United States encourages China to continue down the road of reform and openness, because in this way China's leaders can meet the legitimate needs and aspirations of the Chinese people for liberty, stability, and prosperity. As economic growth continues, China will face a growing demand from its own people to follow the political path of East Asia's modern democracy, adding political freedom to economic freedom. Continuing along this path will contribute to regional and international security....Only by allowing the Chinese people to enjoy these basic freedoms and universal rights can China honor its own constitution and international commitments and reach its full potential. Our strategy seeks to encourage China to make the right strategic choices for its people, while we hedge against other possibilities.[64]

In essence, then, American grand strategy requires China to accept U.S. primacy, and the ideology that underpins it—which means trouble ahead in Sino–American relations.

Although "the United States welcomes a confident, peaceful, and prosperous China that appreciates that its growth and development depends on constructive connections with the rest of the world," the United States is not willing to countenance a China that emerges as a great power rival and challenges American primacy.[65] Unsurprisingly, U.S. grand strategy under both the Bush II and Clinton administrations has aimed at holding down China. While acknowledging that China is a *regional* power, both the Clinton and Bush II administrations have been unwilling to concede that China either is, or legitimately can aspire to be, a world-class great power.[66] Enjoining China against challenging the United States militarily, the Bush II administration's 2002 *National Security Strategy* warns Beijing that "In pursuing advanced military capabilities that can threaten its neighbors in the Asia-Pacific region, China is following an outdated path that, in the end, will hamper its own pursuit of national greatness. In time, China will find that social and political freedom is the only source of that greatness."[67] Washington rejects the notion that China has any justifiable basis for regarding the American military presence in East Asia as threatening to its interests.[68] Defense Secretary Donald Rumsfeld recently reiterated this point when he suggested that any moves by China to enhance its military capabilities are, ipso facto, a signal of aggressive Chinese intent. According to Rumsfeld, China's military modernization cannot possibly be defensive because "no nation threatens China"—a view restated in the Bush II administration's report, *The Military Power of the People's Republic of China*.[69] In the Pentagon's view, "China's military modernization remains ambitious" and in coming years "China's leaders may be tempted to resort to force or coercion more quickly to press diplomatic advantage, advance security interests, or resolve disputes."[70]

The Bush II administration has not entirely abandoned engagement with Beijing, but—more openly than the Bush I and Clinton administrations—it has embraced containment of China as an alternative to engagement. Given the influence of neoconservative foreign policy intellectuals on the administration's grand strategy, this is unsurprising. After all, during the 1990s, leading neoconservatives were part of the so-called Blue Team of anti-China hardliners in the foreign policy community.[71] Containment is a strategy that emphasizes using the traditional hard power tools of statecraft to prevent China's great power emergence and maintain American primacy.[72] The heart of containment, however, lies in military power and alliance diplomacy.

What, specifically, do primacists mean when they call for China's containment? First, they want the United States to pledge explicitly to defend Taiwan from Chinese attack and also to help Taiwan build up its own military capabilities. Primacists believe that the United States should not back away from confronting China over Taiwan and, indeed, they would like the United States to *provoke* such a showdown. They also want the United States to emulate its anti-Soviet Cold War strategy by assembling a powerful alliance of states that share a common interest in curbing rising Chinese power. As part of such a strategy, the United States should tighten its security relationship with Japan and invest it with an overtly anti-Chinese mission. Needless to say, primacists are determined that the United States maintain its conventional and nuclear military superiority over China. Indeed, with respect to nuclear weapons, as Keir Lieber and Daryl Press have pointed out in an important *Foreign Affairs* article, the United States currently has an overwhelming nuclear first-strike capability against China, which will be augmented by the national ballistic missile defense system that the United States currently is deploying. Even if

Beijing switches its military modernization priorities from its current conventional defense buildup to the enhancement of its strategic nuclear deterrent, it will take some time before China could offset the first-strike capability that the United States possesses.

Advocates of containment hope that the various measures encompassed by this strategy will halt China's rise and preserve American primacy.[73] However, as one leading proponent of containment argues, if these steps fail to stop China's great power emergence, "the United States should consider harsher measures."[74] That is, before its current military advantage over China is narrowed, the United States should launch a preventive war to forestall China's emergence as a peer competitor. Of course, in the abstract, preventive war always has been an option in great powers' strategic playbooks—typically as a strategy that declining great powers employ against rising challengers. However, it also is a strategy that also can appeal to a dominant power that still is on top of its game and is determined to squelch potential challengers before they become actual threats.

In fact, preventive war (along with preemptive military strikes) is the grand strategic approach of the Bush II administration, as set out in its 2002 *National Security Strategy* (and reaffirmed by the administration in its 2006 *National Security Strategy)*, and in policy statements by senior administration officials (including President George W. Bush himself). There is nothing in the *logic* of the administration's grand strategy doctrines of preventive war and preemptive action that suggests that it is applicable only to terrorist groups like *al Qaeda* and so-called rouge states (like Iran and North Korea). If anything, preventive strategies should be most appealing with respect to potential rivals like China—those who could become peer competitors of the United States. Here, the pramacists' fixation on defending Taiwan suggests that an American commitment to that island's defense is valued most because it could afford Washington a possible pretext to take on China in a preventive war.

To be sure, the United States should not ignore the potential strategic ramifications of China's arrival on the world stage as a great power. After all, the lesson of history is that the emergence of new great powers in the international system leads to conflict, not peace. On this score, the notion—propagated by Beijing—that China's will be a "peaceful rise" is just as fanciful as claims by American policy-makers that China has no need to build up its military capabilities because it is unthreatened by any other state. Still, this does not mean that the United States and China inevitably are on a collision course that will culminate in the next decade or two in a war. Whether Washington and Beijing actually come to blows, however, depends largely on what strategy the United States chooses to adopt toward China, because the United States has the "last clear chance" to adopt a grand strategy that will serve its interests in balancing Chinese power without running the risk of an armed clash with

Beijing. If the United States continues to aim at upholding its current primacy, however, Sino–American conflict is virtually certain.

There are three elements of current U.S. grand strategy toward China that needed to be reconsidered. The first two are the linked issues of trade and domestic liberalization. Trade is an issue where just about everyone involved in the current debate about America's China policy has gotten it wrong. Engagement—based on economic interdependence and free trade—neither will constrain China to behave "responsibly" nor lead to an evolutionary transformation of China's domestic system (certainly not in any policy-relevant time span). Unfettered free trade simply will accelerate the pace of China's great power emergence: the more China becomes linked to the global economy, the more rapidly it is able to grow in both absolute and relative economic power. To be sure, short of preventive war, there is nothing the United States can do to prevent China from eventually emerging as a great power. Thus, there would be no point in simply ceasing economic relations with China. But the United States must be careful about how—and why—it trades with Beijing.

American trade with China should be driven by strategic, not market, considerations. If Washington cannot prevent China's rise to great power status, it nonetheless does have some control over the pace of China's great power emergence. A U.S. trade policy that helps accelerate this process is shortsighted and contrary to America's strategic interests. The United States must reduce China's export surplus to deprive it of hard-currency reserves that Beijing uses to import high technology and to invest in building up its economic and technological infrastructure (which, in turn, contributes to the modernization of China's military). Washington also should tightly regulate the direct outflow of critical advanced technology from the United States to China in the form of licensing, offset, or joint venture agreements. Individual American corporations may have an interest in penetrating the Chinese market, but there is no *national* interest, for example, in permitting U.S. firms to facilitate China's development of an advanced aerospace industry.

On the other hand, those U.S. hard-liners who want to use Sino–American trade as a bludgeon to compel Beijing to accept America's demands with respect to human rights and democratization also have gotten it wrong: while American leverage is too limited to have any significant positive effects, Washington's attempts to transform China domestically inflame Sino–American relations. America's values are not universally accepted as a model to emulate, least of all by China. Washington's attempts to "export" democracy to China are especially shortsighted and dangerous and have sharpened Sino–American tensions—and strengthened Beijing's resolve to resist U.S. primacy.

Finally, Taiwan is a powder-keg issue in Sino–American relations. China remains committed to national reunification, yet Taiwan is moving perceptibly toward independence. Almost certainly, Beijing would regard a Taiwanese declaration of independence as a *casus belli*. It is unclear how the United

States would respond to a China–Taiwan conflict, although President George W. Bush created a stir in 2001 when he declared that the United States would intervene militarily in the event of a Chinese attack on Taiwan. For sure, however, it is safe to predict that there would be strong domestic political pressure in favor of American intervention. Beyond the arguments that Chinese military action against Taiwan would undermine U.S. interests in a stable world order and constitute "aggression," ideological antipathy toward China and support for a democratizing Taiwan would be powerful incentives for American intervention. On Taiwan, in other words, the arguments of U.S. primacists have come close to locking-in Washington to a potentially dangerous policy.

The primacists' claim that the United States must be prepared to defend Taiwan from Chinese invasion overlooks three points. First, for nearly a quarter century, the United States has recognized that Taiwan is a Chinese province, not an independent state. Second, America's European and Asian allies have no interest in picking a quarrel with China over Taiwan's fate. If Washington goes to the mat with Beijing over Taiwan, it almost certainly will do so alone. (Given their unilateralist bent, however, the prospect of fighting China without allies might not be much concern to American primacists.) Third, by defending Taiwan, the United States runs the risk of armed confrontation with China—probably not in the immediate future, but almost certainly within the next decade or so.

It would be an act of folly for the United States to risk conflict for the purpose of defending democracy in Taiwan. The issue at stake simply would not justify the risks and costs of doing so. Indeed, regardless of the rationale invoked, the contention that the United States should risk war to prevent Beijing from using force to achieve reunification with Taiwan amounts to nothing more than a veiled argument for fighting a "preventive" war against a rising China. If U.S. primacists believe that preventive war is a viable option for coping with a rising China, instead of using Taiwan as a fig leaf they should say so openly so that the merits of this strategy can be debated.

So what should the United States do about China? If the United States persists with its strategy of primacy, the odds of a Sino–American conflict are high. Current American strategy commits the United States to maintaining the geopolitical status quo in East Asia, a status quo that reflects American primacy. The United States' desire to preserve the status quo, however, clashes with the ambitions of a rising China. As a rising great power, China has its own ideas about how East Asia's political and security order should be organized. Unless U.S. and Chinese interests can be accommodated, the potential for future tension—or worse—exists. Moreover, as I already have demonstrated, the very fact of American primacy is bound to produce a geopolitical backlash—with China in the vanguard—in the form of counter-hegemonic balancing. Nevertheless, the United States cannot be completely indifferent to China's rise.

The key component of a new geopolitical approach by the United States would be the adoption of an offshore balancing strategy. Under this approach, a regional East Asian power balance would become America's first line of defense against a rising China and would prevent Beijing from dominating East Asia. The other major powers in Asia—Japan, Russia, India—have a much more immediate interest in stopping a rising China in their midst than does the United States, and it is money in the bank that they will step up to the plate and balance against a powerful, expansionist state in their own neighborhood. It is hardly surprising (indeed, it parallels in many ways America's own emergence as a great power) that China—the largest and potentially most powerful state in Asia—is seeking a more assertive political, military, and economic role in the region, and even challenging America's present dominance in East Asia. This poses no direct threat to U.S. security, however. Doubtless, Japan, India, and Russia (and, perhaps, Korea) may be worried about the implications of China's rapid ascendance, because a powerful China potentially would be a direct threat to *their* security. This is precisely the point of offshore balancing: because China threatens its neighbors far more than it threatens the United States, these neighbors—not the United States—should bear the responsibility of balancing against Chinese power.

Iran   Because of the strategy of primacy and empire, the United States and Iran are on course for a showdown. The main source of conflict—or at least the one that has grabbed the lion's share of the headlines—is Tehran's evident determination to develop a nuclear weapons program. Washington's policy, as President George W. Bush has stated on several occasions—in language that recalls his prewar stance on Iraq—is that a nuclear-armed Iran is "intolerable." Beyond nuclear weapons, however, there are other important issues that are driving the United States and Iran toward an armed confrontation. Chief among these is Iraq. Recently, Zalmay Khalilzad, the U.S. ambassador to Iraq, has accused Tehran of meddling in Iraqi affairs by providing arms and training to Shiite militias and by currying favor with the Shiite politicians who dominate Iraq's recently elected government. With Iraq teetering on the brink of a sectarian civil war between Shiites and Sunnis, concerns about Iranian interference have been magnified. In a real sense, however, Iran's nuclear program and its role in Iraq are merely the tip of the iceberg. The fundamental cause of tensions between the United States and Iran is the nature of America's ambitions in the Middle East and Persian Gulf. These are reflected in current U.S. grand strategy—which has come to be known as the Bush Doctrine. The Bush Doctrine's three key components are rejection of deterrence in favor of preventive/preemptive military action; determination to effectuate a radical shake-up in the politics of the Persian Gulf and Middle East; and gaining U.S. dominance over that region. In this respect, it is hardly coincidental that the administration's policy toward Tehran bears a striking similarity to its policy during the run-up to the March 2003 invasion of Iraq, not only on the nuclear weapons issue but—ominously—with respect to regime change and democratization. This is because the same strategic assumptions that underlay the administration's pre-invasion Iraq policy now are driving its Iran policy. The key question today is whether these assumptions are correct.

In his 2002 State of the Union speech, President George W. Bush famously labeled Iraq and Iran (along with North Korea) as part of the "axis of evil." Just what this meant in strategic terms became apparent in an important address that Bush gave in June 2002 at West Point, in which he announced a new U.S. strategic posture.[75] In that speech, Bush said that the post-9/11 threat to the United States "lies at the crossroads of radicalism and technology"; that is, the ability of rogue states and terrorist groups to obtain weapons of mass destruction (WMD). Throwing nearly a half-century of American strategic doctrine out the window, Bush declared that "Containment is not possible when unbalanced dictators with weapons of mass destruction can deliver those weapons on missiles or secretly provide them to terrorist allies." Henceforth, instead of relying on deterrence and containment, he said, the United States would deal with such threats preemptively. "If we wait for threats to fully materialize," Bush said, "we will have waited too long."

The administration's stance with respect to so-called rogue state threats was amplified in its September 2002 *National Security Strategy.*[76] Here, the offending characteristics of such regimes were defined with specificity. These states "brutalize their own people"; flaunt international law and violate the treaties they have signed; are engaged in the acquisition of WMD, which are "to be used as threats or offensively to achieve the aggressive designs of these regimes"; support terrorism; and "hate the United States and everything it stands for."[77] Given the nature of the threat, the *National Security Strategy* concluded that the Cold War doctrine of deterrence through the threat of retaliation is inadequate to deal with rogue states because the rulers of these regimes are "more willing to take risks, gambling with the lives of their people and the wealth of their nations." Moreover, in contrast to the strategic doctrines of the two superpowers during the Cold War, rogue states purportedly consider WMD to be the "weapons of choice" rather than weapons of last resort.[78] Consequently, the administration argued, rogue states represent a qualitatively different kind of strategic threat, and the United States "cannot remain idle while threats gather." The United States, the administration announced, would adopt a new strategy: "To forestall or prevent such hostile acts by our adversaries, the United States will, if necessary, act preemptively."[79] The preemptive stance of the United States against rogue state threats provided the impetus for the invasion of Iraq and is also driving American policy toward Iran.

If its premises are accepted, the administration's strategy is logical on its own terms. The problem, however, is that the assumptions on which this strategy is based are dubious. First, the administration conflates two *different* threats: the threat from terrorist groups and the threat from so-called rogue states. Terrorist groups like *al Qaeda do* present a novel set of challenges strategically. Precisely because these groups are shadowy, "non-state" actors, it *is* hard to deter them. As is often said, unlike states—rogue or otherwise—terrorist groups have no "return address" to which retaliation can be directed. On the other hand, the threat of retaliation effectively deters states—even rogue states—for several reasons. For one thing, in contrast to terrorist organizations, if a state attacks the United States, Washington knows where to find it—that is, the "return address" is ascertainable—and where to aim a retaliatory strike. Moreover, states can be deterred because, unlike terrorists, they have a lot to lose: if their actions prompt the United States to hit back, a state will suffer devastating damage to its economy, huge loss of life among its citizens, and regime survival will be jeopardized. Jeffrey Record has cut to the heart of the strategic error that confounds the Bush Doctrine:

> Terrorist organizations are secretive, elusive, nonstate entities that characteristically possess little in the way of assets that can be held hostage.... In contrast, rogue states are sovereign entities defined by specific territories, populations, governmental infrastructures and other assets; as such they are more exposed to decisive military attack than terrorist organizations. Or to put it another way, unlike terrorist organizations, rogue states, notwithstanding administration declamations to the contrary, *are subject to effective deterrence and therefore do not warrant status as potential objects of preventive war and its associated costs and risks.*[80]

To put it simply, although there is considerable justification strategically for preempting terrorist threats, there is very little justification for attacking states preemptively or preventively.

The very notion that undeterrable "rogue states" exist is the second questionable assumption on which the administration's strategy is based. In an important article in the Winter 2004/2005 issue of *International Security*, Francis Gavin points out that the post-9/11 era is not the first time that American policy-makers have believed that the United States faced a lethal threat from rogue states.[81] During the 1950s and early 1960s, for example, the People's Republic of China was perceived by Washington in very much the same way as it perceived Saddam Hussein's Iraq, or, currently, Iran. Under the leadership of Chairman Mao Zedong, the Chinese Communist Party imposed harsh repression on China and killed millions of Chinese citizens. Moreover, Beijing—which had entered the Korean War in 1950, menaced Taiwan, gone to war with India in 1962, and seemingly was poised to intervene in Vietnam—was viewed (wrongly) as an aggressive state. For Washington, Mao's China was the poster child of a rogue state, and during the Johnson administration the United States seriously considered launching a preventive war to destroy China's embryonic nuclear program.

In many ways, Mao was seen by U.S. policy-makers as the Saddam Hussein of his time. Moreover, like Iranian president Mahmoud Ahmadi-Nejad—who has made outrageous comments denying the Holocaust and threatening Israel's destruction—Mao also suffered from diarrhea of the mouth. Indeed, Mao arguably was even more afflicted because he trivialized the consequences of nuclear war. Thus—*before* China became a nuclear power (1964)—Mao's rhetoric cavalierly embraced the possibility of nuclear war. "If the worse came to worst and half of mankind died," Mao said, "the other half would remain while imperialism would be razed to the ground and the whole world would become socialist."[82] Once China actually became a nuclear power, however, where nuclear weapons were concerned both its rhetoric and its policy quickly became circumspect and responsible. In fact, a mere five years after the Johnson administration pondered the possibility of striking China preventively, the United States and China were engaged in secret negotiations that, in 1972, culminated in President Richard Nixon's trip to Beijing and Sino–American cooperation to contain the Soviet Union.

The United States' experience with China illustrates an important point: the reasons *states* acquire nuclear weapons are primarily to gain security and, secondarily, to enhance their prestige. This certainly was true of China, which believed its security was threatened by the United States *and* by the Soviet Union. It is also true of Saddam Hussein's Iraq and today's Iran. As Gavin writes, "In some ways, the Kennedy and Johnson administration's early analysis of China mirrors the Bush administration's public portrayal of Iraq in the lead-up to the war. Insofar as Iraq was surrounded by potential nuclear adversaries (Iran and Israel) and threatened by regime change by the most powerful country in the world, Saddam Hussein's desire to develop nuclear weapons may be seen as understandable."[83] The same can be said for Iran, which is ringed by U.S. conventional forces in neighboring Afghanistan and Iraq and in the Persian Gulf, and which also is the target of the Bush II administration's policy of regime change and democratization. Tehran may be paranoid, but in the United States—and Israel—it has real enemies. It is Iran's fear for its security that drives its quest to obtain nuclear weapons.

The same architects of illusion who fulminated for war with Iraq now are agitating for war with Iran. If Iran gets nuclear weapons they say, three bad things could happen: it could trigger a nuclear arms race in the Middle East; it might supply nuclear weapons to terrorists; and Tehran could use its nuclear weapons to blackmail other states in the region or to engage in aggression. Each of these scenarios, however, is improbable in the extreme. During the early 1960s, American policy-makers had similar fears that China's acquisition of nuclear weapons would trigger a proliferation stampede, but these fears did not materialize—and a nuclear Iran will not touch off a proliferation snowball in the Middle East. Israel, of course, already is a nuclear power (as is Pakistan, another regional power). The other three states that might be tempted to go for a nuclear weapons capability are Egypt, Saudi Arabia, and Turkey. As MIT professor Barry Posen points out, however, each of these three states would be under strong pressure *not* do to so.[84] Egypt is particularly vulnerable to outside pressure to refrain from going nuclear because its shaky economy depends on foreign—especially U.S.—economic assistance. Saudi Arabia would find it hard to purchase nuclear weapons or material on the black market—which is closely watched by the United States—and, Posen notes, it would take the Saudis years to develop the industrial and engineering capabilities to develop nuclear weapons indigenously. Turkey is constrained by its membership in NATO and its quest to be admitted to membership of the European Union.

Notwithstanding the near-hysterical rhetoric of the Bush administration and the neoconservatives, Iran is not going to give nuclear weapons to terrorists. This is not to say that Tehran has not abetted groups like Hezbollah in Lebanon, or Hamas in the Palestinian Authority. Clearly, it has. However, there are good reasons that states—even those that have ties to terrorists—draw the line at giving them nuclear weapons (or other WMD): if the terrorists were to use these weapons against the United States or its allies, the weapons could be traced back to the donor state—which would be at risk of annihilation by an American retaliatory strike. Iran's leaders have too much at stake to run this risk. Even if one believed the administration's overheated rhetoric about the indifference of rogue state leaders about the fate of their populations, they do care very much about the survival of their regimes—which means that they can be deterred.

For the same reason, Iran's possession of nuclear weapons will not invest Tehran with options to attack or intimidate its neighbors. Just as it did during the Cold War, the United States can extend its own deterrence umbrella to protect its clients in the region—like Saudi Arabia, the Gulf states, and Turkey. American security guarantees not only will dissuade Iran from acting recklessly but will also restrain proliferation by negating the incentives for states like Saudi Arabia and Turkey to build their own nuclear weapons. Given the overwhelming U.S. advantage in both nuclear and conventional military capabilities, Iran is not going to risk national suicide by challenging America's security commitments in the region. In short, while a nuclear-armed Iran hardly is desirable, neither is it "intolerable," because it could be contained and deterred successfully by the United States.

No serious expert doubts that Tehran is inching closer to developing a nuclear weapons capability. Yet, at least some observers feel that at the end of the day, this crisis—unlike Iraq—will not culminate in war. In part, this is because the United States—perhaps having learned from the Iraq war that there are high diplomatic costs of acting like the Lone Ranger—is working in concert with Britain, France, Germany, and Russia to bring Iran before the bar of world opinion at the United Nations and is asking the international community to impose sanctions on Tehran. Yet, if sanctions are imposed, they are unlikely to be effective. They seldom are. So at the end of the day, the United States will be left with the options of either using military power or acquiescing in a nuclear-armed Iran.

Some observers believe that the Bush II administration has been chastened by its experience in Iraq, and hence will avoid using military force against Iran. It is also commonly argued that the United States has been "overstretched" by its military commitment in Iraq and lacks the ground forces to go to war with Iran. It would be a mistake, however, to conclude that the administration has abandoned the military option. In January 2005, it was reported that since summer 2004 the United States had been mounting reconnaissance missions—using both aerial surveillance and on-the-ground special forces teams—to pinpoint nuclear installations and missile-launching sites inside Iran.[85] There have been recent press reports—including a detailed story by Seymour Hersh in *The New Yorker*—that the Bush administration feverishly is preparing plans for a sustained military campaign against Iran.[86]

Although these efforts could be written off as either routine contingency planning or as a way of supplementing diplomacy with the threat of military action, we should not dismiss the possibility that the administration *really* is contemplating war against Iran. After all, this is a notoriously cloistered administration in which power remains tightly concentrated among a small circle of policy-makers. This is, moreover, an administration whose key policy-makers remain committed to their preexisting worldview. President George W. Bush remains at the apex of this decision-making process, imprisoned in his intellectual bubble and impervious to facts that create cognitive dissonance with his fixed view of the world. We have had ample time to observe Bush's decision-making style, and it seems clear that once his mind is made up, he closes his mind to discrepant facts and stays resolutely—or more accurately, lemming-like—on course. Given his oft-stated view that a nuclear-armed Iran is intolerable, and that Iran is a rogue state, it would be foolish to think the military option is off the table.

But it should be. Attacking Iran would be a strategic blunder of the first magnitude—far worse than going to war with Iraq. To be sure, while the United States may be short of ground troops, it still possesses more than enough air power to mount a sustained bombing campaign against Iran's nuclear facilities. The problem, of course, is that the United States does not know the location of all of Iran's nuclear sites. Consequently, although a bombing campaign probably would inflict enough damage to impose some delay on the Iranian nuclear program, the fact that the United States cannot pinpoint all of Tehran's nuclear facilities means that the United States cannot destroy the Iranian nuclear program or inflict long-term disruption. Simply stated, the United

States ultimately cannot prevent Iran from acquiring nuclear weapons. On the other hand, the risks to the United States in bombing Iran's nuclear infrastructure are high—higher than any benefit that might be gained by slowing down Iran's acquisition of nuclear weapons. Because of its links to the Iraqi Shiites, Iran has the capability to intervene in Iraq and put U.S. forces—and the entire American project there—in even greater jeopardy. Tehran can also use its ties to Hezbollah and Hamas to create instability throughout the region. Indeed, the events of summer 2006 in Gaza and Lebanon suggest that it may be doing so—perhaps to remind the United States that Iran has the capability of responding to any military action that Washington might take in regard to Iran's nuclear programs.

War is always a risky proposition—even for states that have impressive military capabilities. As German Chancellor Theobald Bethamann-Hollweg said during the July 1914 crisis, war is "a leap into the dark"—and a "cosmic roll of the iron dice"—because there are so many imponderables and so many things that can go wrong. This is a lesson that the current administration would do well to take to heart with respect to its Iran policy (and one it should have learned from its experience in Iraq). U.S. military and civilian strategists are so enamored with the idea of using shock and awe to impose America's will on its enemies that they forget what strategy is all about: strategy is a *two*-player game, not a single-player game, in which U.S. adversaries have options of their own. Iran, in fact, has many options because of its links to terrorists, its own military capabilities (which are sufficient to impose high costs should American forces ever launch a ground war against Iran), and the importance of its oil to the global economy.

Iran is in no position to slug it out toe-to-toe against the United States in a conventional military conflict, but it has political, economic, and even diplomatic cards that it can use to make it very costly to the United States to employ military force in an attempt to halt or delay Iran's nuclear weapons program. If the United States does use force against Iran, it will be opposed diplomatically by Europe, China, and Russia. More important, a military strike against Iran would unleash forces that could trigger a true "clash of civilizations" and would make the Persian Gulf and Middle East even more unstable—and more anti-American—than it is now. Simply put—unpalatable though it may be—the military option is not viable with respect to Iran. Still, although a nuclear-armed Iran is not a pleasant prospect, neither is it an intolerable one. Tehran won't be the first distasteful regime to acquire nuclear weapons (nor will it be the last). The United States has adjusted to similar situations in the past and can do so this time. Rather than preventive war and regime change, the best policies for the United States with respect to Iran are the tried and true ones of containment, deterrence, and diplomatic engagement.

The strategy of primacy and empire also calls for the United States to attain dominance in the Middle East by pursuing a policy of regime change with respect to Iran. In February 2006, the administration requested that Congress appropriate $75 million to "support the aspirations of the Iranian people for freedom in their own country."[87] In language eerily reminiscent of that used by the administration during the run-up to the March 2003 invasion of Iraq, President George W. Bush has declared that, "By supporting democratic change in Iran, we will hasten the day when the people of Iran can determine their future and be free to choose their own leaders. Freedom in the Middle East requires freedom for the Iranian people, and America looks forward to the day when our nation can be the closest of friends with a free and democratic Iran." As the administration sees it, the government in Tehran is illegitimate because it is unrepresentative of the Iranian people. As Bush put it, "Iran is a nation held hostage by a small clerical elite that is isolating and repressing its people, and denying them basic liberties and human rights." This is a simplistic view, however—and a dangerous one if it fosters in American policy-makers the expectation that Iranians will welcome U.S.-initiated regime change. All Iranians have long memories of foreign—and especially American—interference in their nation's internal affairs, which is why Washington is not positioned to exploit successfully any political divisions that, in fact, may exist in Iran. Indeed, nothing could be better calculated to trigger a strong Iranian nationalist backlash against the United States than a serious attempt by the administration to orchestrate regime change in Tehran.

The administration's 2006 *National Security Strategy* takes dead aim at Iran, declaring that the United States "may face no greater challenge from a single country than from Iran."[88] The 2006 *National Security Strategy* makes clear that Washington's concerns about Iran go well beyond the nuclear issue: "The Iranian regime sponsors terrorism; threatens Israel; seeks to thwart Middle Eastern peace; disrupts democracy in Iraq; and denies the aspirations of its people for freedom."[89] Finally, the 2006 *National Security Strategy* clearly outlines the administration's view of how U.S.–Iranian tensions can be resolved: "The nuclear issue and our other concerns can ultimately be resolved only if the Iranian regime makes the strategic decision to change those policies, open up its political system, and afford freedom to its people. This is the ultimate goal of U.S. policy."[90] The policy of seeking regime change and democratization in Iran is based on the same faulty premises that have led the United States into the morass in Iraq. To understand the dangers that could lie ahead in Iran, it is necessary to revisit the road to war and occupation in Iraq.

The Wages of the American Empire: The Iraqi Quagmire

The March 2003 invasion of Iraq and the subsequent—still ongoing—occupation is the most damning indictment of American Empire. The decision to invade Iraq was the inevitable consequence of the triumph within the Bush II administration's policy-making councils of the ideas—and ideology—that the neoconservative architects of empire had been purveying since the early 1990s.

As such, Iraq demonstrates powerfully the illusions upon which the American Empire is based. As a consequence of these imperial fantasies, the United States blundered into an avoidable war—a war with disastrous consequences, the full dimensions of which will become clear only with the passage of time.

Wilsonianism and American Security   Hard power is the backbone of American primacy. But liberal ideology is the foundation upon which the new American Empire is built. "Wilsonianism" is the shorthand term for the projection abroad of America's domestic liberal ideology. Realism and liberalism often are viewed by foreign policy analysts as polar opposite approaches to U.S. foreign policy. However, the American Empire joins realism and liberalism together like Siamese twins. For sure, U.S. policy-makers *are*—and always have been—concerned about power and security. But Wilsonian ideology has a lot to say both about the purposes for which America's power is used and about how its security requirements are conceptualized. The American Empire rests on the belief that to be secure, the United States must spread democracy abroad—if necessary, by force. For the United States, a world comprised of democracies will be peaceful, stable, and safe ideologically—or so it is claimed.[91] By spreading democracy abroad, the American Empire is supposed to bolster America's security from external threat, *and*—at least as important—to ensure the integrity of America's liberal domestic institutions, which is considered to be tied inextricably to their replication abroad. As the diplomatic historian Walter LaFeber has observed, "America's mission" of extending democracy worldwide is not altruistic. Rather, "it grew out of the belief that American liberties could not long exist at home unless the world was made safe for democracy," and thereby for America's own economic system, which was held to be the very foundation of its domestic political system.[92] Of course, the dark side of this view of America's security requirements is the belief that the United States can be secure *only* in a world composed of democratic states. As diplomatic historian Lloyd C. Gardner notes, the key assumption underlying U.S. strategic and foreign policy is that "America must have a favorable climate for its institutions to thrive, and perhaps even for them to survive."[93]

The belief that the export of democracy is crucial to American security was a key component of U.S. grand strategy during the Bush I and Clinton administrations. Indeed, the democratic enlargement—the active promotion by the United States of democracy abroad—was the centerpiece of Clinton administration's foreign policy. If anything, the Wilsonian notion of spreading democracy has played an even more salient role in the Bush II administration's grand strategy than it did during the two preceding administrations. In its 2002 *National Security Strategy*, the Bush II administration committed the United States to promoting a "balance of power that favors freedom" and declared that it would extend democracy "to every corner of the world."[94] It stated that U.S. grand strategy would be "based on a distinctly American internationalism that reflects the union of our values and our national interests."[95] As the administration explained, this means that U.S. grand strategy "must start" from America's "core beliefs and look outward for possibilities to expand liberty."[96] In his January 2004 State of the Union speech, President George W. Bush proclaimed that "America is a nation with a mission" and that its aim is "a democratic peace."[97]

The 2006 version of its *National Security Strategy of the United States* reaffirms the primacy of democracy promotion in the administration's grand strategy. Echoing the views of the Clinton administration, the 2006 strategy document states that the United States: "cannot pretend that our interests are unaffected by states' treatment of their own citizens. America's interest in promoting effective democracies rests on an historical fact: states that are governed well are most inclined to behave well."[98] The administration believes that America's strategic interests are congruent with its Wilsonian ideology. As the 2006 *National Security Strategy* states:

> Championing freedom advances our interests because the survival of liberty at home increasingly depends on the success of liberty abroad. Governments that honor their citizens' dignity and desire for freedom tend to uphold responsible conduct toward other nations, while governments that brutalize their people also threaten the peace and stability of other nations. Because democracies are the most responsible members of the international system, promoting democracy is the most effective long-term measure for strengthening international stability; reducing regional conflicts; countering terrorism and terror-supporting extremism; and extending peace and prosperity.[99]

Reflecting the influence of the neoconservative apostles of Empire, the Bush II administration regards the Middle East's democratic transformation as the antidote to Islamic extremism and terrorism.

Attributing the terrorist threat to the United States to the failure of democracy to take root in the Middle East, President George W. Bush has committed the United States to "a forward strategy of freedom in that region."[100] Both President Bush and Condoleezza Rice have made clear their belief that, while it is a formidable and prolonged challenge—a "generational commitment"—the Middle East's successful democratization is crucial to American security.[101] As Bush has put it:

> Sixty years of Western nations excusing and accommodating the lack of freedom in the Middle East did nothing to make us safe—because in the long run, stability cannot be purchased at the expense of liberty. As long as the Middle East remains a place where freedom does not flourish, it will remain a place of stagnation, resentment, and violence ready for export. And with the spread of weapons that can bring catastrophic

harm to our country and to our friends, it would be reckless to accept the status quo.[102]

Rice has argued that the Middle East suffers from a "freedom deficit." Because of this, she says, "it is a region where hopelessness provides a fertile ground for ideologies that convince promising youths to aspire not to a university education, career, or family, but to blowing themselves up—taking as many innocent lives with them as possible. These ingredients are a recipe for great instability, and pose a direct threat to American security."[103] The administration is committed to its own version of the domino theory in the Middle East. It believes that a democratic Iraq will trigger a wave of democratization throughout the Middle East. As Bush has put it: "The failure of Iraqi democracy would embolden terrorists around the world, increase dangers to the American people, and extinguish the hopes of millions in the region. Iraqi democracy will succeed—and that success will send forth the news, from Damascus to Tehran—that freedom can be the future of every nation. The establishment of a free Iraq at the heart of the Middle East will be a watershed event in the global democratic revolution."[104] This is why the administration believes the stakes in Iraq are so high.

Regime Change and Democratization: The Bush II Administration's Real Reasons for Invading Iraq   Doubtless, the apostles of Empire will seek to exculpate themselves with a "revisionist" view of the war and the decisions that led up to it. They will claim that the decision to invade was correct; the United States could have defeated the insurgency and attained its larger aims in the region had not American strategy been hamstrung by poor planning and execution. The truth, however, is different: the American decision to use military force to overthrow Saddam Hussein and achieve regime change in Iraq was irredeemably flawed in its conception. The imperial project of democratizing Iraq, and using it as a springboard to transform the entire Middle East politically, was doomed from the outset. There are many things that we know now about the Iraq war—things that were known—or should have been known—during the run-up to the invasion. First, as John Mearsheimer and Stephen Walt pointed out in an important prewar article in *Foreign Policy* magazine, the U.S. policy of containing and deterring Saddam Hussein was working—which also was the pre-invasion view of the U.S. intelligence community.[105] There was no chance that Saddam Hussein's Iraq was going to attack either the oil-producing states of the Persian Gulf or Israel (the security of which often seemed to weigh more heavily in the calculations of the American Empire's neoconservative architects than did the national interests of the United States). Second, although in an attempt to rally public support for Iraq policy the administration repeatedly suggested there was a link between Saddam Hussein and 9/11, this patently was not true. Amazingly, however, the administration continues to rely on this false canard to justify its decision to invade Iraq. As the administration's 2006 *National Security Strategy* says, in its view it "inherited an Iraq threat that was unresolved," and "for America, the September 11 attacks underscored the danger of allowing threats to linger unresolved."[106] Third, there were no weapons of mass destruction. The administration's intimations—notably by Bush, Cheney, and Rice—that the United States needed to strike Iraq preventively to ensure that the American homeland itself did not fall victim to an Iraqi nuclear strike was conjured out of whole cloth. History will judge harshly as prevarications the administration's tales of mushroom clouds, aluminum tubes, and Nigerian yellow cake—tales it told to mislead the American people into supporting a disastrous and unnecessary war in pursuit of the administration's imperial delusions in the Middle East.

Of course, the administration still likes to say that "everyone"—not just the U.S. intelligence community, but also the intelligence services of America's allies—believed that Saddam Hussein had chemical and biological weapons and was attempting to acquire nuclear weapons. However, here, the administration overlooks two inconvenient facts. One is that if the administration had allowed the UN weapons inspectors more time to complete their task, it would have become evident that Iraq had no WMD capabilities. The other is that the Bush administration did not *want* the inspections to continue precisely because it was concerned that the inspectors would discover the truth about the nonexistence of Iraqi WMD, and thereby undercut the rationale for embarking on a war it already had decided to fight regardless of whether Iraq possessed WMD. For the same reason, the administration twisted the U.S. intelligence community's findings on Iraqi WMD to suit its own political purposes.

Paul R. Pillar, who served as National Intelligence Officer for the Near East and South Asia from 2000 to 2005 has written that the intelligence community's evidence—admittedly flawed—about Iraqi WMD played no part in the administration's decision to go to war. The administration, he says, already had decided to go to war and was interested only in intelligence analysis that supported its decision. Indeed, we now know from several sources that from its first days in office, Iraq was high on the administration's strategic agenda, and that within hours of the 9/11 attacks, leading administration officials wanted to use the terrorist strikes on New York and Washington, D.C., as a pretext to attack Iraq.[107] For this reason, the administration also simply ignored the consensus of the intelligence community that the United States would face grave postwar difficulties if it occupied Iraq.[108] There is ample evidence now that, in terms of explaining the administration's decision to go to war, the issue of Iraqi WMD was a red herring. For example, Deputy Defense Secretary Paul Wolfowitz has stated that regardless of whether Iraq possessed weapons of mass destruction, the invasion was justified, because "We have an important job to do in Iraq, an absolutely critical job to do, and that is to help the Iraqi people to build a free and democratic country."[109]

Thanks to the "Downing Street Memoranda"—which chronicle the pre-war discussions between British and Bush administration officials—we know that as early as March 2002 regime change, indeed, was the real aim of the administration's policy. However, in both Washington and London, officials doubted that the case for war with Iraq could be sold politically on that basis. Elimination of Iraqi WMD was the most politically saleable argument for invading Iraq, and this is the argument—along with the alleged link between Saddam Hussein and 9/11—the Bush administration invoked to win support for the war, the real objective of which was to overthrow Saddam Hussein and to democratize Iraq as the catalyst to a broader democratic transformation throughout the Middle East region.[110] Indeed, in July 2002, British intelligence warned that "Bush wanted to remove Saddam, through military action, justified by the conjunction of terrorism and WMD." The British also noted that the administration's "case was thin. Saddam was not threatening his neighbors and his WMD capability was less than that of Libya, North Korea, or Iran."[111] President George W. Bush himself has made it clear that WMD was not the factor that drove U.S. policy toward Iraq. In a December 2005 speech—after conceding that prewar intelligence estimates about Iraqi WMD were "wrong"—Bush said that "it wasn't a mistake to go into Iraq. It was the right decision to make":

> Given Saddam's history and the lessons of September the 11th, my decision to remove Saddam Hussein was the right decision. Saddam was a threat—and the American people and the world is [sic] better off because he is no longer in power. We are in Iraq today because our goal has always been more than the removal of a brutal dictator; it is to leave a free and democratic Iraq in its place. As I stated in a speech in the lead-up to the war, a liberated Iraq could show the power of freedom to transform the Middle East by bringing hope and progress to the lives of millions. So we're helping the Iraqi—Iraqi people build a lasting democracy that is peaceful and prosperous and an example for the broader Middle East.[112]

During a press conference several days later, Bush reiterated that, although the intelligence information about Iraqi WMD was incorrect, his decision to remove Saddam Hussein was "right" because the administration's "broader strategic objective" was the "establishment of democracy."[113]

In seeking to democratize Iraq—and the Middle East—the administration embarked upon "Mission Impossible" (not "Mission Accomplished," as the administration prematurely crowed in May 2003). The administration ought to have known this, because there were plenty of authoritative *prewar* warnings of the difficulties the United States would encounter if it invaded—and occupied—Iraq. In November 2002, James Fallows wrote an article in *The Atlantic Monthly* about the post-conflict challenges the United States most likely would face after defeating Iraq. His article was based on numerous interviews with policy experts. The broad conclusion of those with whom he spoke was that "the day after a war ended, Iraq would become America's problem, for practical and political reasons. Because we would have destroyed the political order and done physical damage in the process, the claims on American resources and attention would be comparable to those of any U.S. state."[114] In the short term, Fallows noted, the United States would face the difficult task of imposing order in what probably would be a chaotic environment. In the longer term, the United States would confront enormous obstacles in setting up an Iraqi government and in keeping Iraq from fracturing along sectarian lines. As Fallows noted, some senior administration officials and their neoconservative acolytes in the foreign policy community expected that Saddam Hussein's overthrow would be the catalyst to spread of democracy throughout the Arab world. However, among the experts that he interviewed, "the transforming vision is not, to put it mildly, the consensus among those with long experience in the Middle East."[115]

Fallows's conclusions were supported by other studies. For example, before the war, an independent working group cosponsored by the Council on Foreign Relations and Rice University's James A. Baker Institute for Public Policy warned that "There should be no illusions that the reconstruction of Iraq will be anything but difficult, confusing, and dangerous for everyone involved."[116] In contrast to the Panglossian hopes of administration officials—notably Deputy Secretary of Defense Paul Wolfowitz—that revenues from the sale of Iraqi oil would cover the costs of postwar reconstruction, the working group presciently warned that because of prewar deterioration and war-inflicted damage, there would be no oil "bonanza" in postwar Iraq. Moreover, the costs of postwar reconstruction of Iraq's economy would be steep. Finally, the working group warned that "The removal of Saddam…will not be the silver bullet that stabilizes" the Middle East.[117]

Perhaps the most prescient study of the travails the United States would face was a paper written by two analysts at the U.S. Army War College's Strategic Studies Institute. Although the apostles of Empire famously predicted that American troops would be greeted as liberators by the Iraqis, the authors of the Army War College report knew this was a pipe dream:

> Most Iraqis and most other Arabs will probably assume that the United States intervened in Iraq for its own reasons and not to liberate the population. Long-term gratitude is unlikely and suspicion of U.S. motives will increase as the occupation continues. A force initially viewed as liberators can rapidly be relegated to the status of invaders should an unwelcome occupation continue for a prolonged period of time.[118]

The authors highlighted the probability that U.S. occupation forces would find themselves facing guerilla and terrorist attacks—or even a large-scale insurrection.[119] The report also stressed that "the establishment of democracy or even some sort of rough pluralism in Iraq, where it has never really existed previously, will be a staggering challenge for any occupation force seeking to govern in a post-Saddam era.[120] Ethnic and sectarian tensions, the authors noted, not only would constitute a formidable obstacle to Iraq's democratization, but also could lead to the breakup of a post-Saddam Iraq. The report also warned that the costs of rebuilding Iraq would be substantial, and that these could not be covered by Iraqi oil revenues. The authors' bottom line was that, "The possibility of the United States winning the war and losing the peace in Iraq is real and serious."[121]

The Army War College report was hardly the lone voice within the government predicting that the United States would confront a monumental post-war task if it invaded Iraq. The U.S. intelligence community counseled the administration to refrain from going to war and forecast that if did invade, the United States would face a "messy aftermath in Iraq."[122] The intelligence community also believed that a postwar Iraq: "would not provide fertile ground for democracy; would witness a struggle for power between Sunnis and Shiites; and would require 'a Marshall Plan–type effort' to rebuild the nation's economy."[123] Events have underscored the prescience of the Army War College's, and the intelligence community's, estimates of the probable course of events in postwar Iraq.

The argument has been made—notably in George Packer's recent book, *The Assassins' Gate*—that the United States' failure in Iraq is not attributable to the nature of the administration's goals, but rather the result of the Pentagon's top civilian leadership's cavalier indifference to planning for the post-conflict occupation of Iraq.[124] There is a kernel of truth to this argument, because the willful failure of the Defense Department's civilian leaders to prepare adequately for the occupation bordered on criminal negligence. As a July 2002 memorandum prepared by British officials for Prime Minister Tony Blair noted, the United States was giving "little thought" to dealing with a post-conflict Iraq notwithstanding that "a postwar occupation of Iraq could lead to costly and protracted nation-building."[125] Still, even with the best planning in the world, it is unlikely that the United States could have succeeded in democratizing Iraq. The administration had no understanding of the issues and challenges involved in democratic transformations. If it had, it surely would have realized both that Iraq was singularly unsuitable candidate for democratization and that America's power to effectuate a region-wide democratic transformation was limited, while the risks of embarking on such a policy were sobering. To put it slightly differently, promoting—or imposing—democracy on other states is a daunting task, and American interests are *not* served by a policy of democracy promotion.

Democratizing Iraq: The Test Case of the American Empire   Before the invasion, administration officials pretty much believed that the processes of democratization and nation-building in Iraq would be a piece of cake. They frequently invoked the examples of post-1945 Germany and Japan as "proof" that the United States could export democracy to Iraq without undue difficulty. For at least three reasons, they should have known better: the use of military force by outside powers to impose democracy rarely works; military occupations seldom are successful; and the preconditions for a successful democratic transformation did not exist in Iraq. Democracy and nation-building are hard tasks, and Washington's track record is not encouraging.[126] Since the Cold War's end, the United States—without any notable success—has engaged in democracy promotion and nation-building in Panama, Somalia, Haiti, Bosnia, Kosovo, and Afghanistan. U.S. efforts to assist post-Soviet Russia's democratization—a key American aim since the Cold War's end—also have been disappointing. The lesson to be learned from these efforts is that, even under the best conditions, the barriers to transplanting democracy successfully on foreign soil are formidable. This is no surprise to those scholars who study democratic transitions. They know that successful democratic transitions invariably are the product of domestic factors.[127] That is, the push for democracy must come from within the state making the transition rather than being imposed by an outside power.[128] In this respect, the post–World War II American occupations of Germany and Japan stand out as notable exceptions to the rule, and thus have little relevance in predicting the outcome of the U.S. democratization effort in Iraq.

Those who have studied military occupations know that the odds of success are stacked against occupying powers. As David Edelstein observes:

> Military occupations usually succeed only if they are lengthy, but lengthy occupations elicit nationalist reactions that impede success. Further, lengthy occupation produces anxiety in imperialist occupation powers that would rather withdraw than stay. To succeed, therefore, occupiers must both maintain their own interest in a long occupation, and convince an occupied population to accept extended control by a foreign power. More often than not, occupiers either fail to achieve those goals, or they achieve them only at a high cost.[129]

The successful U.S. occupations of Germany and Japan—which helped both nations emerge from the ashes of World War II as prosperous and stable democracies—succeeded because of unique circumstances that enabled the United States to attain its goal of transforming Germany and Japan politically. Similar circumstances do not exist in Iraq, however. In contrast to Iraq, the United States was able to impose order and stability swiftly upon the defeated Germans and Japanese. Both of the Axis powers were utterly defeated and shattered societies; surrendered unconditionally; and were occupied by an overwhelming number of American (and, in Germany's case, Allied) troops. In Japan, moreover, Emperor Hirohito commanded the Japanese people to surrender and to cooperate with the occupation authorities. Furthermore, as Edelstein points out, "Whereas war-weary Germans and Japanese recognized the need for an occupation to help them rebuild, a significant portion of the Iraqi people have never welcomed the U.S.-led occupation as necessary."[130] Finally, as Edelstein also notes, the Cold War was a hugely important factor contributing to the success of two post–World War II occupations. Both the Germans and the Japanese felt threatened by the Soviet Union, and they recognized their need to align with the United States in order to be safeguarded against the Soviet menace. In postwar Iraq, no such external threat exists to bind the United States and the Iraqis together. On the contrary, the leaders of Iraq's dominant Shiite population gravitate toward Iran.

Among those who study democratic transitions there is widespread agreement about the factors that conduce successful democratic transitions. These include a modern market-based economy; absence of hostility between ethnic or religious groups; a political culture that is hospitable to democracy; and a vibrant civil society.[131] Another important factor is the capacity of state institutions to perform their tasks effectively. Iraq met none of these criteria. As Andrew Rathmell has observed: "Iraq was not a promising environment for achieving the goal of building a peaceful, democratic, free-market nation. Iraq had failed to develop into a cohesive nation-state; its state structures had the form but not the substance of a modern state; its economy was in poor shape; and its society had endured almost half a century of debilitating violence."[132]

From this perspective it's no wonder that the American Empire has foundered in its democratization and nation-building effort in Iraq. Iraq was nothing like post–World War II Japan and Germany. In the wake of World War II, the United States could aspire to transform Germany and Japan into democracies because there was a strong foundation upon which to build.[133] Both the defeated Axis powers had the internal prerequisites in place for a successful democratic transformation and consolidation. First, Germany and Japan both had political cultures that were hospitable to democracy. Before 1933, after all, Germany actually had been a practicing democracy. And while Japan was not, it had both substantial experience with parliamentary government and exposure to liberal ideas. Second, wartime devastation notwithstanding, Germany and Japan both had advanced economies and a substantial middle class. Third, both Germany and Japan were essentially homogenous societies. Neither was afflicted with any serious power struggles between rival ethnic, national, or religious groups. Fourth, in both Germany and Japan, there were effective state institutions that the United States was able to reform and reconstitute, and to which power then could be transferred.

With respect to each of these factors, Iraq is an altogether different kettle of fish. Since it was created out of the post–World War I ruins of the Ottoman Empire, Iraq has had no experience with democracy, and there is nothing to suggest that its political culture is conducive to democracy. Second, Iraq's economy was a shambles even before March 2003 (the result of Iraq's long war with Iran, the 1991 Gulf War, and the UN-mandated economic sanctions imposed after the 1991 war). Third, Iraq is a seething cauldron of ethnic and sectarian conflict in which Kurds, Sunni Arabs, and Shiite Arabs are battling for power. Indeed, as many of the administration's critics predicted before the war, the U.S. invasion and occupation have opened a Pandora's box of ethnic and sectarian strife in Iraq and brought it to the brink of civil war, and—perhaps—disintegration as a unitary national state. Moreover, as Robert Dahl points out, the building of democratic institutions can be side-tracked by the intervention of outside powers that are pursuing their own political agendas.[134] Turkey, Saudi Arabia, the Gulf States, Syria, and Iran all have important interests at stake in postwar Iraq and are likely to meddle there by exploiting Iraq's ethnic and sectarian fault lines. Fourth, in Iraq there are no effective state institutions that the United States can reconstitute. These will have to be built from scratch, and there are no signs that the United States has been successful in doing so. Iraqi politics and government are characterized by corruption and the ongoing struggle for power among the Shiites, Sunnis, and Kurds. The "sovereign" Iraqi state remains unable to fulfill the most basic definition of a state: it has failed to attain a monopoly on the legitimate use of force and has been unable to impose order and stability in Iraq. In part, this is because key state institutions—like the military and police—are dominated by private (Shiite) militias. In short, no one should hold his breath waiting for the emergence of a democratic Iraq. In truth, there never was a snowball's chance that the architects of Empire could achieve their goal of successfully democratizing Iraq, and if they had based U.S. policy on a careful study of both democratic transitions generally, and Iraqi history specifically, instead of reflexive ideology, they would have realized this. Instead, they led the United States into the geopolitical quicksand of Iraq.

Conclusion: Imperial Illusions

The American Empire rests on two foundations. One is the *faux* realism of primacy. The other is Wilsonian ideology. The apostles of Empire argue that by maintaining American primacy, and by exporting democracy abroad, the United States can attain peace and security. As I have argued elsewhere, however, the peace promised by the American Empire is a peace of illusions.[135]

Primacy is a strategy that causes *in*security because it will lead to a geopolitical backlash against the United States. In time, this will take the form of traditional great power counterbalancing against American primacy. The emergence of new great powers during the next decade or two is all but certain. Indeed, China already is on the cusp of establishing itself as a peer competitor to the United States. The U.S. grand strategy of maintaining its global primacy has put the United States on the road to confrontation with a rising China, and with Iran. In the short term, primacy has triggered asymmetric responses—notably terrorism—in regions like the Middle East where America's geopolitical presence is resented.

Wilsonian ideology drives the American Empire because its proponents posit that the United States must use its military power to extend democracy abroad. Here, the ideology of Empire rests on assumptions that are not supported by the facts. One reason the architects of Empire champion democracy promotion is because they believe in the so-called democratic peace theory, which holds that democratic states do not fight other democracies. Or as President George W. Bush put it with his customary eloquence, "democracies don't war; democracies are peaceful."[136] The democratic peace theory is the probably the most overhyped and undersupported "theory" ever to be concocted by American academics. In fact, it is not a theory at all. Rather it is a theology that suits the conceits of Wilsonian true believers—especially the neoconservatives who have been advocating American Empire since the early 1990s. As serious scholars have shown, however, the historical record does not support the democratic peace theory.[137] On the contrary, it shows that democracies do not act differently toward other democracies than they do toward nondemocratic states. When important national interests are at stake, democracies not only have threatened to use force against other democracies, but, in fact, democracies *have gone to war* with other democracies.

The Bush administration and the neoconservative imperialists believe that by democratizing the Middle East, the United States will solve the problem of terrorism and bring stability to the region. There are three things wrong with this vision of American Empire in the Middle East. First, democratization is not the magic bullet cure for terrorism. A policy of regime change—using U.S. overt military power or covert capabilities to oust governments in the Middle East and install new regimes that will clamp down on radical Islam—is misdirected and will *not* make the United States safer. Radical Islam is fueled by resentment against American primacy; specifically, the U.S. military presence in the region. The expansion of that presence for the purpose of overthrowing regimes does not make America more secure from terrorist attacks. On the contrary, it simply adds fuel to terrorist groups like *al Queda*. As Robert Pape observes:

> Spreading democracy at the barrel of a gun in the Persian Gulf is not likely to lead to a lasting solution against suicide terrorism. Just as al-Qaeda's suicide terrorism campaign began against American troops on the Arabian Peninsula and then escalated to the United States, we should recognize that the longer that American forces remain in Iraq, the greater the threat of the next September 11 from groups who have not targeted us before. Even if our intentions are good, the United States cannot depend on democratic governments in the region to dampen the risk of suicide terrorism so long as American forces are stationed there.[138]

Second, the United States lacks the capabilities to democratize the region. As Brent Scowcroft has said: "The reason I part with the neocons is that I don't think in any reasonable time frame the objective of democratizing the Middle East can be successful. If you can do it, fine, but I don't think you can, and in the process of trying to do it you can make the Middle East a lot worse."[139] Third, the administration and its neoconservatives should be careful what they wish for in the Middle East.

Even if the American Empire does bring about regime change and "democratization" in the Middle East, we probably will rue the consequences. As Katarina Delacoura points out, "democratization in the Arab world may have a number of outcomes unpalatable for the US."[140] The electoral victory of the radical Hamas organization in the February 2006 Palestinian elections—coupled with the strong showing of the fundamentalist Islamic Brotherhood in Egypt's 2005 parliamentary elections—proves the point: the United States is likely to be very displeased with the outcomes of democratic elections in the region. Indeed, the Bush administration was so upset with the victory of Hamas that it reportedly discussed with Israel a policy to destabilize the Palestinian Authority in order to force Hamas out of power.[141] The overthrow of autocratic regimes will make the region even less stable than it currently is. Governments like Saudi Arabia's may be distasteful, but there is truth to the adage that the devil one knows is better than the devil one does not know. For all of America's Wilsonian traditions, the wisest of U.S. statesmen have accepted that the real world is not neatly divided between good regimes and bad ones, and that sometimes American interests are best served by dealing with nondemocratic regimes. This is especially true in a region like the Middle East where, as Lawrence Freedman reminds us, "the real alternatives are chaos or autocracy."[142]

Simply put, American efforts to export democracy easily may backfire. Why? Because *ill*-liberal democracies usually are unstable and often adopt ultranationalist and bellicose external policies.[143] As Edward D. Mansfield and Jack Snyder have pointed out, "Pushing countries too soon into competitive electoral politics not only risks stoking war, sectarianism and terrorism, but it also makes the future consolidation of democracy more difficult."[144] Far from leading to the touted (but illusory) "democratic peace" that is so near and dear to the hearts of American imperialists, "unleashing Islamic mass opinion through sudden democratization might raise the likelihood of war."[145] Moreover, in a volatile region like the Middle East, it is anything but a sure bet that newly democratic regimes—which, by definition would be sensitive to public opinion—would align themselves with the United States. And, if new democracies in the region should fail to satisfy the political and economic aspirations of their citizens—precisely the kind of failure to which new democracies are prone—they easily could become a far more dangerous breeding ground for terrorism than are the authoritarian (or autocratic/theocratic) regimes now in power in the Middle East.

Iraq has been the first test case of the new American Empire, and the Bush administration and neoconservative architects of Empire have flunked. Far from creating a stable democracy in Iraq, they have created chaos. At best, Iraqi "democracy" will result in a pro-Iranian Shiite regime that will be hostile to the United States (and to Israel). At worst, Iraq will fragment along ethnic and sectarian lines and plunge into civil war—a war that could draw in Iraq's neighbors and cause regional instability that is worse by an order of magnitude than the instability that prevailed in the region before March 2003. Finally, the imperial adventure in Iraq has both distracted the United States from the real war against the terrorist perpetrators of 9/11 and simultaneously increased U.S. vulnerability to terrorism. President Bush has stated repeatedly that Iraq is "the central front on the war on terrorism." But, if this is the case now, it was *not* before March 2003. There was *no* connection between *al Qaeda* and Iraq. Iraq only became a haven for terrorists *after* the American invasion—an invasion, as Bush's own CIA Director Porter Goss said, that served to heighten the terrorist threat to the United States.[146] One huge disaster is enough—more than enough—for any grand strategy. American Empire is a failed strategy. The time has come for the United States to adopt a new grand strategy that will avoid the errors of Empire, and actually enhance—rather than weaken—American security.

Notes

1. Max Boot, "The Case for American Empire," *The Weekly Standard*, October 15, 2001, pp. 28–30. As Boot put it, "Afghanistan and other troubled lands today cry out for the sort of enlightened foreign administration once provided by self-confident Englishmen in jodhpurs and pith helmets."
2. Ibid., p.30.
3. Ibid.
4. Michael H. Hunt, *Ideology and U.S. Foreign Policy* (New Haven, Conn.: Yale University Press, 1987), p. 42.
5. Michael Hogan, *A Cross of Iron: Harry S. Truman and the Origins of the National Security State, 1945–1954* (Cambridge, UK: Cambridge University Press, 1998), pp. 8, 15.
6. This argument is developed in Christopher Layne, *The Peace of Illusions: American Grand Strategy from 1940 to the Present* (Ithaca, N.Y.: Cornell University Press, 2006).
7. William Kristol and Robert Kagan, "Toward a Neo-Reaganite Foreign Policy," July/August 1996, *Foreign Affairs* 75 (4): 20.
8. Ibid., p. 23.
9. Ben Wattenberg, "Peddling 'Son of Manifest Destiny'," *Washington Times*, 21 March 1990, quoted in Claes G. Ryn, "The Ideology of American Empire," *Orbis* (Summer 2003), p. 388.
10. Charles Krauthammer, "The Unipolar Moment Revisited," *The National Interest*, 70 (Winter 2002/03): 13.
11. Kristol and Kagan, "Toward a Neo-Reaganite Foreign Policy," p. 23.
12. Zalmay Khalilzad, "Losing the Moment? The United States and the World after the Cold War," *Washington Quarterly* 18 (2): 94.
13. Ibid.
14. Dick Cheney, *Defense Strategy for the 1990s: The Regional Defense Strategy* (Washington, D.C.: Department of Defense, January 1993), p. 6.

15. "Remarks by Dr. Condoleezza Rice to the International Institute for Strategic Studies," London, England, June 26, 2003, www.whitehouse.gov/news/releases/2003/06/print/20030626. html.

16. *The National Security Strategy of the United States of America* (Washington, D.C.: The White House, September 2002), www.whitehouse.gov/nsc/nss.pdf.

17. Patrick E. Tyler, "U.S. Strategy Plan Calls for Insuring No Rivals Develop," *New York Times*, March 8, 1992, p. A1.

18. "Excerpts from Pentagon's Plan: 'Prevent the Re-emergence of a New Rival,'" *New York Times*, March 8, 1992, p. A14 (emphasis added).

19. *The National Security Strategy of the United States* (2002), (emphasis added).

20. Bill Clinton, "Remarks to the American Society of Newspaper Editors," April 1, 1993 (emphasis added), http://clinton6.nara.gov/1993/04/1993-04-01-presidents-speech-to-am-soc-of-newspaper-editors.html.

21. Press Conference by President Bill Clinton, Hong Kong, July 3 1998, http://clinton4.nara. gov/WH/New/China/19980703-22272.html.

22. James Mann, *The Rise of the Vulcans: The History of Bush's War Cabinet* (New York: Viking, 2004), p. xii.

23. "President's State of the Union Message to Congress and the Nation," *New York Times*, January 21, 2004, p. A14.

24. Richard A. Van Alstyne, *The Rising American Empire* (New York: W.W. Norton, 1974), p. 1.

25. Robert Kagan and William Kristol, "The Present Danger," *The National Interest* 59 (Spring 2000), p. 62; Kristol and Kagan, "Toward a Neo-Reaganite Foreign Policy," p. 27.

26. Kagan and Kristol, "The Present Danger," Ibid., p. 64.

27. Letter to President Clinton on Iraq, January 26, 1998, http://www.newamericancentury. org/iraqclintonletter.htm.

28. Charles Krauthammer, "The Real New World Order: The American Empire and the Islamic Challenge," *The Weekly Standard*, November 12, 2001, p. 27.

29. Charles Krauthammer, "In Defense of Democratic Realism," *The National Interest* 77 (Fall 2004), p. 15.

30. Mann, *The Rise of the Vulcans*, p. 353.

31. Ibid., p. 24.

32. On offensive realism, see John J. Mearsheimer, *The Tragedy of Great Power Politics* (New York: W.W. Norton, 2001); Layne, *The Peace of Illusions*.

33. Mearsheimer, *Tragedy of Great Power Politics*, p. 33.

34. Henry A. Kissinger, "The Long Shadow of Vietnam," *Newsweek*, 1 May 2000, p. 50.

35. William C. Wohlforth, "The Stability of a Unipolar World," *International Security* 24 (1) (Summer 1999): 4–41.

36. Paul Kennedy, *The Rise and Fall of the Great Powers: Economic Change and Military Conflict from 1500 to 2000* (New York: Random House, 1987), p. 533.

37. *Mapping the Global Future: Report of the National Intelligence Council's 2020 Project* (Washington, D.C.: Government Printing Office, December 2004), p. 47.

38. The Strategic Assessment Group's analysis of current and projected world power shares was based on the International Futures Model developed by Barry Hughes. For a discussion of methodology and summary of the Strategic Assessment Group's findings, see Gregory F. Treverton and Seth G. Jones, *Measuring National Power* (Santa Monica, Calif.: RAND Corporation, 2005), pp. iii, ix–x.

39. Michael Mandelbaum, *The Case for Goliath: How America Acts as the World's Government in the 21st Century* (New York: PublicAffairs, 2005), p. xvi.

40. Michael Mandlebaum, "David's Friend Goliath," *Foreign Policy* 152 (January/February 2006), pp. 50–56.

41. Quoted in Demetri Sevastopulo, "Rumsfeld Signals Wish to See Allies Take Reins," *Financial Times*, February 3, 2006.

42. Stephen M. Walt, "Keeping the World 'Off-Balance': Self-Restraint and U.S. Foreign Policy," in G. John Ikenberry, ed., *America Unrivaled: The Future of the Balance of Power* (Ithaca, N.Y.: Cornell University Press, 2002), p. 139 (emphasis in original.)

43. Joseph S. Nye Jr., "The Power We Must Not Squander," *The New York Times*, January 3, 2000. On the role of soft power in American grand strategy, see Joseph S. Nye Jr., *Bound Lead: The Changing Nature of American Power* (New York: Basic Books, 1990); Joseph S. Nye Jr., *The Paradox of American Power: Why the World's Only Superpower Can't Go It Alone* (New York: Oxford University Press, 2002), especially chaps. 1 and 5; Joseph S. Nye Jr., *Soft Power: The Means to Success in World Politics* (New York: Public Affairs, 2004).

44. G. John Ikenberry and Charles A. Kupchan, "The Legitimation of Hegemonic Power," in David P. Rapkin, ed., *World Leadership and Hegemony* (Boulder, Colo.: Lynne Rienner, 1990), p. 52.

45. Joshua Murvachik, *The Imperative of American Leadership: A Challenge to Neo-Isolationism* (Washington, D.C.: AEI Press, 1996), p. 34.

46. Cheney, *Defense Strategy for the 1990s*, p. 7.

47. G. John Ikenberry, "Strategic Reactions to American Preeminence: Great Power Politics in the Age of Unipolarity," Report to the National Intelligence Council, July 28, 2003, http://www.dni.gov/nic/confreports_stratreact.html, p.35.

48. Glen Frankel, "Opposition to U.S. Policy Grows in Europe," *Washington Post*, September 4, 2004, p. A4; Craig Kennedy and Marshall M. Bouton, "The Real Trans-Atlantic Gap," *Foreign Policy* 133 (November/December 2002), pp. 64–74; see Daniel M. Nelson, "Transatlantic Transmutations," *Washington Quarterly* 25 (4): 51–66; Special Report, "American Values: Living with a Superpower," *The Economist*, January 4, 2002. A recent Harris survey found that Europeans See the United States as a greater threat to international stability than either China or Iran. John Thornhill, David Dombey, and Edward Allen, "Europeans see U.S. as Greater Threat to Stability than Iran," *Financial Times*, June 19, 2006. I am grateful to Gabriela Marin Thornton for calling my attention to both the *Washington Post* story and the Nelson article.

49. Paul Sharp, "Virtue Unrestrained: Herbert Butterfield and the Problem of American Power," *International Studies Perspectives* 5 (3): 300–315.

50. Anonymous (Michael Scheuer), *Imperial Hubris: Why the West Is Losing the War on Terror* (Washington, D.C.: Brassey's, 2004), p. xviii.

51. Bruce Hoffman, *Inside Terrorism* (New York: Columbia University Press, 1998), pp. 14–15. Also see James D. Kiras, "Terrorism and Irregular Warfare," in John Bayliss et al., *Strategy in the Contemporary World: An Introduction to Strategic Studies* (New York: Oxford University Press 2002), pp. 228–229.

52. Karl von Clausewitz, *On War*, ed. and trans. Michael Howard and Peter Paret, (Princeton, N.J.: Princeton University Press, 1976), p. 92.

53. Richard K. Betts, "The New Threat of Mass Destruction," *Foreign Affairs* 77 (1) (January–February 1998), p. 41. Betts was referring to the first attack on the World Trade Center in 1993.

54. The term "blowback" is borrowed from Chalmers Johnson, *Blowback: The Costs and Consequences of the American Empire* (New York: Metropolitan Books, 2000).

55. Anonymous, *Imperial Hubris*, p. 8.

56. Robert A. Pape, *Dying to Win* (New York: Random House, 2005), p. 4.

57. Ibid.

58. Anonymous, *Imperial Hubris*, p. 8.

59. William S. Cohen, *The United States Security Strategy for the East Asia–Pacific Region* (Washington, D.C.: Department of Defense, 1998), p. 30. As Deputy Secretary of State Robert Zoellick put it, the United States wants China to become "a responsible stakeholder" in the international system. Robert B. Zoellick, "Remarks to the National Committee on U.S.–China Relations," September 21, 2005, www.state.gov/p/eap/rls/rm/.

60. Bill Clinton, "Remarks by President Clinton and President Jiang Zemin in Exchange of Toasts," The White House, October 29, 1997 http://clinton6.nara.gov/1999/09/1999-09-11-remarks-by-president-clinton-and-president-jiang.html; William Cohen, "Annual Bernard Brodie Lecture," University of California, Los Angeles, October 28, 1998. www.defenselink.mil/speeches/1998/s19981106-secdef.html; *U.S. Security Strategy for the East-Asia Pacific Region* (1998), As National Security Adviser Berger put it: "Our interest lies in protecting our security while encouraging China to make the right choices"—especially choosing to allocate its resources to internal development rather than building up its military power. Samuel R. Berger, "American Power: Hegemony, Isolation, or Engagement," Address to the Council on Foreign Relations, Washington, D.C., October 21, 1999, http://clinton5.nara.gov/WH/EOP/NSC/html/speeches/19991021.html.

61. Zoellick, "Remarks to National Committee."
62. "President Discusses Freedom and Democracy in Kyoto, Japan,"http://www.whitehouse.gov/news/releases/2005/11/images/20051116-6_d-0577-5156.html1-44.6KB.
63. Ibid.
64. *The National Security Strategy of the United States of America* (Washington, D.C.: The White House, March 2006), pp. 41–42.
65. Zoellick, "Remarks to National Committee."
66. For example, Defense Secretary William Cohen described China as an Asian power. Cohen, "Annual Bernard Brodie Lecture."
67. This is another example of "American exceptionalism." Obviously, U.S. policy-makers believe that the admonition that the pursuit of modern military capabilities is an "outdated path" that runs counter to achieving true national greatness applies only to others, and not to the United States.
68. *The U.S. Security Strategy for the East–Asia Pacific Region* (1998).
69. Remarks Delivered by Secretary of Defense Donald H. Rumsfeld, Shangri-La Hotel, Singapore, June 4, 2005, http://www.defenselink.mil/speeches/2005/sp20050604-secdef1561.html; Office of the Secretary of Defense, *Annual Report to Congress: The Military Power of the People's Republic of China* (Washington, D.C., Department of Defense, 2005), p. 13, http://www.defenselink.mil/news/Jul2005/d20050719china.pdf.
70. Apparently, however—at least in the Pentagon's view—America's overwhelming military power never tempts the United States "to resort to force or coercion more quickly to press diplomatic advantage, advance security interests, or resolve disputes." Ibid., p. 14.
71. Robert G. Kaiser and Steven Mufson, "'Blue Team' Draws a Hard Line on Beijing," *Washington Post*, Februrary 22, 2000, p. A1.
72. The most comprehensive recent statement of the hard-line containment strategy—upon which this discussion is based—is Bradley A. Thayer, "Confronting China: An Evaluation of Options for the United States," *Comparative Strategy* 24 (1): 71–98.
73. Keir A. Lieber and Daryl G. Press, "The Rise of U.S. Nuclear Primacy," *Foreign Affairs*, 85 (2) (March/April 2006), http://www.foreignaffairs.org/2006/2.html.
74. Thayer, "Confronting China," p. 93.
75. "President Bush Delivers Graduation Speech at West Point," June 1, 2002, http://www.whitehouse.gov/news/releases/2002/06/print/20020601-3.html.
76. *National Security Strategy of the United States* (2002).
77. Ibid., pp. 13–14.
78. Ibid., p. 15.
79. Ibid.
80. Jeffrey Record, *Bounding the Global War on Terrorism* (Carlisle Barracks, Pa.: United States Army War College, Strategic Studies Institute, December 2003), pp. 16–17 (emphasis in original).
81. Francis J. Gavin, "Blasts from the Past: Proliferation Lessons from the 1960s," *International Security* 29 (3): 100–135.
82. Ibid., p. 101.
83. Ibid., p. 135.
84. Barry R. Posen, "We Can Live with a Nuclear Iran," *New York Times*, February 27, 2006, http://www.nytimes.com/2006/02/27/opinion/27posen.html.
85. "U.S. Has Reportedly Sent Teams into Iran," *Los Angeles Times*, January 17, 2005, p. A3.
86. Seymour Hersh, "Iran Plans," *The New Yorker*, April 17, 2006, www.newyorker.com/fact/content/articles/060417fa_fact; Philip Sherwell, "U.S. Prepares Nuclear Blitz against Iran's Nuclear Sites," *Daily Telegraph*, February 13, 2006, http://news.telegraph.co.uk/news/main.jhtml?xml=/news/2006/02/12/wiran12.xml.
87. Secretary of State Condoleezza Rice, Testimony before the Senate Foreign Relations Committee, February 15, 2006, http://www.state.gov/secretary/rm/2006/61209.htm; Glenn Kessler, "Rice Asks for $75 Million to Increase Pressure on Iran," *Washington Post*, 16 February 2006, p. A1.
88. *National Security Strategy* (2006), p. 20.
89. Ibid.
90. Ibid.

91. This belief is widely held by academic students of IR and of American foreign policy and has been pretty well summed up by Tufts University political scientist Tony Smith. As he puts it, the American national interest properly rests on the liberal internationalist belief "that only a world that respects the right of democratic self-determination, fosters nondiscriminatory markets, and has institutional mechanisms to ensure the peace can be an international order ensuring the national security and so permitting liberty at home." Tony Smith, *America's Mission: The United States and the Worldwide Struggle for Democracy in the Twentieth Century* (Princeton, N.J.: Princeton University Press, 1994), p. 327.

92. Walter LaFeber, *America, Russia, and the Cold War* (New York: McGraw-Hill, 1997), p. 235.

93. Lloyd C. Gardner, *A Covenant with Power: America and World Order from Wilson to Reagan* (New York: Oxford University Press, 1984), p. 27.

94. *National Security Strategy* (2002), pp. 2–3.

95. Ibid., p. 3.

96. Ibid., p. 4.

97. "President's State of the Union Message to Congress and the Nation," *New York Times*, 21 January 2004, p. A14.

98. *National Security Strategy of the United States* (2006), p. 36.

99. Ibid., p. 3.

100. "Remarks by the President at the 20th Anniversary of the National Endowment for Democracy," November 6, 2003, http://www.whitehouse.gov/news/releases/2003/11/print/20031106-3.html, p. 5.

101. "Remarks by Condoleezza Rice, Assistant to the President for National Security Affairs, to the Chicago Council on Foreign Relations," October 8, 2003, http://www.whitehouse.gov/news/releases/2003/10/print/20031008-4.html.

102. "Remarks by the President at the 20th Anniversary of The National Endowment for Democracy."

103. Remarks to the Chicago Council on Foreign Relations." Bush has underscored the administration's dedication to achieving a democratic transformation in the Middle East and has linked this objective to U.S. national security. "As long as the Middle East remains a place of tyranny, despair, and anger," he said, "it will continue to produce men and movements that threaten the safety of America and our friends." "President's State of the Union Message to Congress and the Nation."

104. "Remarks by the President at the 20th Anniversary of The National Endowment for Democracy."

105. See Walter Pincus, "Ex-CIA Official Faults Use of Date on Iraq," *Washington Post*, February 10, 2006, p. A1.

106. Ibid., p. 23.

107. For example, see Ron Suskind, *The Price of Loyalty: George W. Bush, the White House, and the Education of Paul O'Neill* (New York: Simon & Schuster, 2004); Bob Woodward, *Plan of Attack* (New York: Simon & Schuster, 2004); Bob Woodward, *Bush at War* (New York: Simon & Schuster, 2002).

108. See Pincus, "Ex-CIA Official Faults Use of Date on Iraq."

109. Quoted in Thom Shanker, "Wolfowitz Defends War, Illicit Iraqi Arms or Not," *New York Times*, February 1, 2004, p. A8.

110. John Daniszewski, "New Memos Detail Early Plans for Invading Iraq, *Los Angeles Times*, June 15, 2005, www.latimes.com/news/nationworld/nation/la-fg-britmemos-15jun15,0,7062164.story?coll=la-home-headlines

111. Walter Pincus, "British Intelligence Warned Blair of War," *Washington Post*, May 13, 2005, p. A18.

112. President Discusses Iraqi Elections, Victory in the War on Terror. Washington, D.C., The Woodrow Wilson Center, December 14, 2005, http://www.whitehouse.gov/news/releases/2005/12/20051214-1.html.

113. Press Conference of the President, December 19, 2005, http://www.whitehouse.gov/news/releases/2005/12/print/20051219-2.html.

114. James Fallows, "The Fifty-First State?" *Atlantic Monthly*, November 2002, http://www.theatlantic.com/doc/print/200211/fallows.

115. Ibid.

116. *Guiding Principles for U.S. Post-Conflict Policy in Iraq: Report of an Independent Working Group Cosponsored by the Council on Foreign Relations and the James A. Baker III Institute for Public Policy of Rice University* (New York: Council on Foreign Relations, 2003), p. 3.
117. Ibid., p. 14.
118. Conrad C. Crane and W. Andrew Terrill, *Reconstructing Iraq: Insights, Challenges, and Missions for Military Forces in a Post-Conflict Scenario* (Carlisle Barracks, Pa.: U.S. Army War College, Strategic Studies Institute, February 2003), pp. 18–19.
119. Ibid., pp. 34–39.
120. Ibid., p. 23.
121. Ibid., p. 42.
122. Pincus, "Ex-CIA Official Faults Use of Date on Iraq."
123. Ibid.
124. Clearly, the Pentagon failed abysmally to plan for the occupation of Iraq. For discussion, see Michael R. Gordon and Bernard E. Trainor, *Cobra II: The Inside Story of the Invasion and Occupation of Iraq* (New York: Pantheon, 2006).
125. Walter Pincus, "Memo: U.S. Lacked Full Postwar Iraq Plan," *Washington Post*, June 12, 2005, p. A1.
126. Even some of the strongest proponents of democratic enlargement acknowledge that the task is hard, and the prospects of enduring success are low. For example, in his survey of cases where the United States has tried to export democracy, the political scientist Tony Smith concedes that America's record in the Philippines, the Caribbean, and Central and Latin America essentially is one of failure. Smith, *America's Mission*, pp. 58–59.
127. Juan J. Linz and Alfred Stepan, *Problems of Democratic Transition and Consolidation: Southern Europe, South America, and Post-Communist Europe* (Baltimore: Johns Hopkins University Press, 1996), p. 73.
128. After reviewing the relative importance of external versus internal influences on successful democratic consolidation, Whitehead concludes that "internal factors were of primary importance in determining the course and outcome of the transition attempt, and international factors played a secondary role." Laurence Whitehead, "International Aspects of Democratization," in Guillermo O'Donnell, Philippe C. Schmitter, and Laurence Whitehead, eds., *Transitions from Authoritarian Rule: Comparative Perspectives* (Baltimore: Johns Hopkins University Press, 1986), p. 4.
129. David Edelstein, "Occupational Hazards: Why Military Occupations Succeed or Fail," *International Security* 29 (1): 50–51.
130. Ibid., p. 51.
131. This list is based on Robert Dahl, *On Democracy* (New Haven, Conn.: Yale University Press, 1998), p. 147; Samuel P. Huntington, *The Third Wave: Democratization in the Late Twentieth Century* (Norman: University of Oklahoma Press, 1981), pp. 37–38.
132. Andrew Rathmell, "Planning Post-Conflict Reconstruction in Iraq: What Can We Learn," *International Affairs* 81 (5): 1018.
133. On the U.S. occupation of Germany, see John Gimbel, *The American Occupation of Germany: Politics and the Military, 1945–1949* (Stanford, Calif.: Stanford University Press, 1968); Richard L. Merritt, *Democracy Imposed: U.S. Occupation Policy and the German Public, 1945–1949* (New Haven, Conn.: Yale University Press, 1995); Edward N. Peterson, *The American Occupation of Germany: Retreat to Victory* (Detroit: Wayne State University Press), pp. 341–343; Thomas Alan Schwarz, *America's Germany: John J. McCloy and the Federal Republic of Germany* (Cambridge, Mass.: Harvard University Press, 1991). Robert Wolfe, ed., *Americans as Proconsuls: United States Military Government in Germany and Japan, 1944–1954* (Carbondale: Southern Illinois University Press, 1984). On the American occupation of Japan, see John W. Dower, *Embracing Defeat: Japan in the Wake of World War II* (New York: W.W. Norton, 2000); Howard B. Schonberger, *Aftermath of War: Americans and the Remaking of Japan, 1945–1952* (Kent, Ohio: Kent State University Press, 1989); Robert E. Ward and Sakimoto Yoshikazu, *Democratizing Japan: The Allied Occupation* (Honolulu: University of Hawaii Press, 1987); and Wolfe, ed., *Americans as Proconsuls*.
134. Dahl, *On Democracy*, p. 147.
135. Layne, *The Peace of Illusions*.
136. "Press Conference of the President," December 19, 2005.

137. See Layne, "Kant or Cant? The Myth of the Democratic Peace," *International Security,* 19 (2) (Fall 1994), pp. 5–49; Christopher Layne, "Shell Games, Shallow Gains, and the Democratic Peace," *International History Review* 19 (4): 4; Henry Farber and Joanne Gowa, "Polities and Peace," *International Security* 20 (2) (Winter 1996/97): 123–146; David Spiro, "The Insignificance of the Liberal Peace," *International Security* 19 (2) (Fall 1994): 50–86.

138. Robert A. Pape, *Dying to Win: The Strategic Logic of Suicide Terrorism* (New York: Random House, 2005), p. 246.

139. Jeffrey Goldberg, "Breaking Ranks," *The New Yorker,* October 31, 2005, http://www.newyorker.com/printables/fact/051033lfa_ct2.

140. Katarina Delacoura, "US Democracy Promotion in the Arab Middle East since 11 September 2001," *International Affairs* 81 (5): 975.

141. Steven Erlanger, "U.S. and Israelis Are Said to Talk of Hamas Ouster," *New York Times,* February 14, 2006, http://www.nytimes.com/2006/02/14/international/middleeast/14mideast.html.

142. Lawrence Freedman, "A Legacy of Failure in the Arab World," *Financial Times,* January 26, 2004, p. 13.

143. On ill-liberal democracies, see Fareed Zakaria, "The Rise of Illiberal Democracy," *Foreign Affairs* 76 (6) (November/December 1997): 22–43. For rebuttals to Zakaria, see John Shattuck and J. Brian Atwood, "Why Democrats Trump Autocrats," *Foreign Affairs* 77 (2) (March/April 1998): 167–170; Marc F. Plattner, "Liberalism and Democracy: Can't Have One without the Other," *Foreign Affairs* 77 (2) (March/April 1998): 171–180. On the war-proneness of newly democratizing states, which, in contrast to "mature" democracies, usually are ill-liberal, see Edward D. Mansfield and Jack Snyder "Democratization and the Danger of War," *International Security* 20 (1) (Summer 1995): 5–38.

144. Edward D. Mansfield and Jack Snyder, "Prone to Violence: The Paradox of the Democratic Peace," *The National Interest* 82 (Winter 2005/06): 39.

145. Ibid, p. 41.

146. In February 2005, Goss stated: "Islamic extremists are exploiting the Iraqi conflict to recruit new anti-U.S. jihadists. These jihadists who survive will leave Iraq experienced and focused on acts of urban terrorism. They represent a potential pool of contacts to build transnational terrorist cells, groups and networks in Saudi Arabia, Jordan, and other countries." Quoted in Dana Priest and Josh White, "War Helps Recruit Terrorists, Hill Told: Intelligence Officials Talk of Growing Insurgency," *Washington Post,* February 17, 2005, p. A1.

3

Reply to Christopher Layne
The Strength of the American Empire

BRADLEY A. THAYER

During World War I, the French statesman Gorges Clemenceau famously defended his right to direct his country's military affairs over the objections of the military. He is often quoted as saying "War is too serious a matter to entrust to military men." I would like to amend that: American grand strategy is too serious a matter to entrust solely to academics, or politicians and policy-makers, or issue-advocates and lobbyists. It is the proper purview of all Americans and is too serious a business to entrust to anyone but them. The spirit that animates this book is that the American people, as well as people in other countries, should understand the costs and benefits of American grand strategy and debate the grand strategic alternatives available to the United States.

This book is an effort to promote understanding of the grand strategy of the United States, its grand strategic options, as well as the benefits and risks associated with them. Layne and I are powerful advocates of alternative grand strategies, but we join each other in recognizing the importance of this debate and in our desire to foster it. We recognize that Americans can and will disagree about the proper role of the United States in international politics and how best to advance and defend the interests of the United States.

To advance these goals, in this chapter I would like to respond to Layne's criticisms of the grand strategy of primacy made in chapter 2 and present some final reflections on the grand strategy of offshore balancing versus the grand strategy of primacy. I argue that primacy is the superior grand strategic choice for the United States because it provides the greatest benefit for the United States with the least risk. Furthermore, to abandon the grand strategy of primacy at this time would entail enormous dangers for the United States and its allies.

Why Layne's Critique of American Primacy Is Wrong

Layne levels several major allegations against the grand strategy of primacy, and I want to respond to the two most important: first, that the pursuit of primacy makes the United States less secure; second, that Iraq serves as a test case for the American Empire, and—he submits—it is a test that the United States is failing. Before I reply, I would like to thank Layne for illuminating the risks associated with primacy. Although both of his charges are wrong—in fact, the pursuit of hegemony makes the United States more secure and Iraq reflects some of the best principles of the United States—having Layne present the case against the American Empire helps to advance this vital debate.

Layne does not illuminate the risks associated with his preferred grand strategy of offshore balancing principally because those risks far outweigh any gain. Abandoning primacy in favor of offshore balancing would entail enormous dangers for the United States and its allies. Most importantly, it would cause the United States to abandon its dominant position in favor of inferiority for the first time in a century. Offshore balancing is a radical break with American tradition, statecraft, and policies which have allowed the United States first, to defeat four peer competitors—Germany, Italy, Japan, and the Soviet Union in World War II and the Cold War; second, by peaceful means, to replace the previously dominant state—Great Britain; and third, to win greater security for the American people and their allies.

U.S. Power Makes the United States More, Not Less, Secure

There is a category of events in life: Things that almost never happen. Included in this are rich people complaining that they have too much money, athletes saying they are too strong, Hollywood stars bemoaning that they receive too much publicity, and countries asserting they have too much power and want less.

Countries want more power to protect their people and their other interests, such as economic growth and allies. Layne is right about a fundamental cause—the anarchy of the international system. But there is a debate among theorists of international relations concerning whether states should adopt a "Goldilocks" strategy—having just enough power, not too little nor too much—or if they should maximize their power to the extent that they are able to do so.[1] Defensive realists like Layne favor a "Goldilocks" strategy for security. Offensive realists, like me, favor maximizing power for security. For the United States, defensive realists are more passive, support a smaller military, and favor reducing its commitments abroad. Offensive realists are more active, support a larger military, and favor using the power of the United States to protect its interests overseas, e.g., by taking the fight to the terrorists in the Middle East rather than waiting for them to come to the United States to attack Americans.

Each country knows it will never be perfectly secure, but that does not detract from the necessity of seeking security. International politics is a dangerous environment in which countries have no choice but to participate. Any involvement—from the extensive involvement of the United States to the narrow activity of Switzerland—in this dangerous realm runs the risk of a backlash. That is simply a fact of life in international politics. The issue is how much participation is right. Thankfully, thus far the United States recognizes it is much better to be involved so that it may shape events, rather than to remain passive, having events shaped by other countries, and then adjusting to what they desire.

In contrast to Layne's argument, maximizing the power of the United States aids its ability to defend itself from attacks and to advance its interests. This argument is based on its prodigious economic, ideological, and military power. Due to this power, the United States is able to defeat its enemies the world over, to reassure its allies, and to dissuade states from challenging it. From this power also comes respect and admiration, no matter how grudging it may be at times. These advantages keep the United States, its interests, and its allies secure, and it must strive to maintain its advantages in international politics as long as possible.

Knowing that American hegemony will end someday does not mean that we should welcome or facilitate its demise; rather the reverse. The United States should labor to maintain hegemony as long as possible—just as knowing that you will die someday does not keep you from planning your future and living today. You strive to live as long as possible although you realize that it is inevitable that you will die. Like good health, Americans and most of the world should welcome American primacy and work to preserve it as long as possible.

The value of U.S. power for the country itself as well as for most of the world is demonstrated easily by considering four critical facts about international politics. First, if you doubt that more power is better, just ask the citizens of a country that has been conquered, like the Czech Republic, Poland, Kuwait, or Lebanon; or the citizens of a country facing great peril due to external threats or terrorists, like Colombia, Georgia, Israel, Nepal, or Turkey. These countries would prefer to possess greater power to improve their security. Or query the citizens of a fallen empire. For the British, French, or Russians, having the power to influence the direction of international politics, having the respect and recognition that flows from power, and, most importantly, having the ability to advance and defend their country's interests are elements of power that are missed greatly. In sum, the world looks very different from the perspective of these countries than it does from a powerful and secure United States.

Second, U.S. power protects the United States. That sentence is as genuine and as important a statement about international politics as one can make. International politics is not a game or a sport. There are no "time outs," there is no halftime and no rest. It never stops. There is no hiding from threats and dangers in international politics. If there is no diplomatic solution to the threats it confronts, then the conventional and strategic military power of the United States is what protects the country from such threats. Simply by declaring that the United States is going home, thus abandoning its commitments or making half pledges to defend its interests and allies, does not mean that others will respect its wishes to retreat. In fact, to make such a declaration implies weakness and emboldens aggression. In the anarchic world of the animal kingdom, predators prefer to eat the weak rather than confront the strong. The same is true in the anarchic realm of international politics. If the United States is not strong and does not actively protect and advance its interests, other countries will prey upon those interests, and even on the United States itself.

Third, countries want to align themselves with the United States. Far from there being a backlash against the United States, there is worldwide bandwagoning with it. The vast majority of countries in international politics have alliances with the United States. There are approximately 192 countries in the world, ranging from the size of giants like Russia to Lilliputians like Vanuatu. Of that number, you can count with one hand the countries opposed to the United States—China, Cuba, Iran, North Korea, and Venezuela. Once the leaders of Cuba and Venezuela change, there is every reason to believe that those countries will be allied with the United States, as they were before their present rulers—Fidel Castro and Hugo Chavez—came to power. North Korea will collapse someday, removing that threat, although not without significant danger to the countries in the region. Of these states, only China has the potential power to confront the United States. The potential power of China should not be underestimated, but neither should the formidable power of the United States and its allies.

There is an old saying that you can learn a lot about someone by looking at his friends (or enemies). It may be true about people, but it is certainly true of the United States. Of the 192 countries in existence, a great number, 84, are allied with the United States, and they include almost all of the major economic and military states.

This includes twenty-five members of NATO (excluding the United States—Belgium, Bulgaria, Canada, Czech Republic, Denmark, Estonia, France, Germany, Greece, Hungary, Iceland, Italy, Latvia, Lithuania, Luxembourg, Netherlands, Norway, Poland, Portugal, Romania, Slovakia, Slovenia, Spain, Turkey, and the United Kingdom); fourteen major non-NATO allies (Australia, Egypt, Israel, Japan, South Korea, Jordan, New Zealand, Argentina, Bahrain, Philippines, Thailand, Kuwait, Morocco, and Pakistan); nineteen Rio Pact members (excluding Argentina and Venezuela—The Bahamas, Bolivia, Brazil, Chile, Colombia, Costa Rica, Dominican Republic, Ecuador, El Salvador, Guatemala, Haiti, Honduras, Mexico, Nicaragua, Panama, Para-

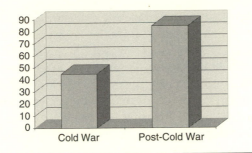

Figure 3.1 Number of U.S. allies.

guay, Peru, Trinidad and Tobago, and Uruguay); seven Caribbean Regional Security System members (Antigua and Barbuda, Barbados, Dominica, Grenada, Saint Christopher and Nevis, Saint Lucia, Saint Vincent and the Grenadines), and thirteen members of the Iraq coalition who are not captured by the other categories: Albania, Armenia, Azerbaijan, Bosnia and Herzegovina, Fiji, Georgia, Kazakhstan, Macedonia, Moldova, Mongolia, Singapore, Tonga, and Ukraine. In addition, Afghanistan, Iraq, Kyrgyzstan, Saudi Arabia, Tajikistan, and Tunisia are now important U.S. allies.

This is a ratio of almost 17 to 1 (84 to 5) of the countries allied with the United States against those who are opposed to it. And other states may be added to the list of allies. For example, a country like Nigeria is essentially pro–United States although there is no formal security arrangement between those countries. This situation is unprecedented in international politics— never have so many countries been aligned with the dominant state in modern history.

As Figure 3.1 demonstrates, it is a big change from the Cold War when most of the countries of the world were aligned either with the United States (approximately forty-five) or the Soviet Union (about twenty-four countries),

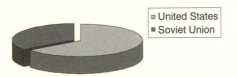

Figure 3.2 Ratio of alliances during the Cold War. 1.8:1 in favor of the United States.

which yields a ratio of 1.8 to 1 of states aligned with the United States to those

Figure 3.3 Ratio of states aligned with the United States to those opposed to it in the post–Cold War period. 17:1 in favor of the United States.

of the Soviet Union, as captured by Figure 3.2. Figure 3.3 illuminates the ratio of states aligned with the United States to those opposed to it in the post–Cold War period.

So, while we are entitled to our own opinions about international politics, we not entitled to our own facts. They must be acknowledged. In the post–Cold War world, the United States is much better off—it is much more powerful and more secure—than was during the Cold War.

What is more, many of the allies of the United States have become more dependent on the United States for their security than during the Cold War. For many years now, most NATO countries have only spent a fraction of their budget on defense, and it is not transparent how they would defend themselves if not for the United States did not. Only six of the twenty-five members of NATO (not counting the United States) are spending 2 percent or more of their GDP on defense, while nineteen spend less than 2 percent. Such a low level of defense spending is possible only because of the security provided by the United States.

The fourth critical fact to consider is that the security provided by the power of the United States creates stability in international politics. That is vitally important for the world, but easily forgotten. Harvard professor Joseph Nye often compares the security provided by the United States to oxygen. If it were taken away, a person would think of nothing else. If the security and stability provided by the United States were taken away, most countries would be much worse off, and arms races, vicious security competition, and wars would result. It would be a world without NATO or other key U.S. alliances. We can imagine easily conflict between traditional rivals like Greece and Turkey, Syria and Israel, India and Pakistan, Taiwan and China, Russia and Georgia, Hungary and Romania, Armenia and Azerbaijan, and an intense arms race between China and Japan. In that world, the breakup of Yugoslavia would have been a far bloodier affair that might have escalated to become another European war. In contrast to what might occur absent U.S. power, we see that the post–Cold War world dominated by the United States is an era of peace and stability.

The United States does not provide security to other countries because it is altruistic. Security for other states is a positive result (what economists call a positive externality) of the United States pursuing its interests. Therefore, it would be a mistake to seek "benevolence" in great power politics. In international politics, states advance their self-interest and, most often, what might appear to be "benevolent" actions are undertaken for other reasons. To assist Pakistani earthquake refugees, for example, is benevolent but also greatly aids the image of the United States in the Muslim world—so self-interest is usually intertwined with a humanitarian impulse.

The lesson here is straightforward: Countries align themselves with the United States because to do so coincides with their interests, and they will continue to do so only as long as their interests are advanced by working with Uncle Sam. In 1848, the great British statesman Lord Palmerston captured this point best when he said: "We have no eternal allies and we have no perpetual enemies. Our interests are eternal and perpetual, and those interests it is our duty to follow."[2]

It is important to know what other countries think of the United States, but, equally, it is a fundamental mistake to worry disproportionately about what the rest of the world thinks. Leaders lead. That may be unpopular at times, indeed, perhaps most of the time. A cost of leadership is that the leader will be criticized for doing too much, or for accomplishing too little. But at the same time, few states would want to replace the leadership of the United States with the leadership of China. The allies of the United States are precisely its allies because to be so serves the interests of these countries. One country does not align itself with another for reasons of sentiment or emotion.

If the United States adopted offshore balancing, many of those allies would terminate their relationship with the United States. They would be forced to increase their own armaments, acquire nuclear weapons, and perhaps ally against the United States, even aiming their nuclear weapons at the United States. In those circumstances, the United States would be far less secure and much worse off than it is now.

That might be the future if the United States changed its grand strategy. To be sure, at present the United States is a great ally. It is rich and powerful, with many allies all over the world. It weilds enormous influence in international institutions as well. When a global problem arises, countries turn to the United States to solve it.

When you reflect on all the countries who have been hegemons, the United States is the most accommodating and helpful the world has seen. That is a weighty point and must be emphasized—too frequently, it is not. The United States is so for many reasons, including its democratic ideology, the good-natured qualities of the American people, and geography; and the United States is far away from the Eurasian and African landmasses, which makes it a more attractive ally for a typical country in Eurasia—say, Poland or Turkey—since the United States must be invited in comparison to a great power like Russia. If Warsaw or Ankara were to invite the Russians in, they may never leave, and they might incorporate Poland or Turkey into Russia. There is no danger of that with the United States. And this simple fact alone helps us enormously in our relations with the rest of the world.

The Success of Iraq: An Ally of the United States, Not Its Clone

When we deal with major events in international politics, time is often needed to yield a context one does not see at the time. In military history, for example, many generals and admirals thought they had lost when the reverse was true. Jimmy Doolittle thought he was going to face a court martial immediately after his raid on Japan in April 1942. He saw the raid as a failure because none of the aircraft survived, all crash-landing in or near China. He did not realize that he had lifted the morale of the entire country during a dark time when there was nothing but defeat. After World War II, the occupations of West Germany and Japan were perceived as confused and muddled affairs. However, we now know the occupations placed Germany and Japan on the path to become the vibrant democracies and economic powerhouses they are now. There is a similar perception of failure in Iraq in the minds of many Americans.

This should not be a surprise, since much of the American media persistently shows a country of bombings and chaos. Most Americans do not have the time to get their news from other, more objective sources that illuminate the good, the bad, and the ugly in Iraq, rather than just the bad (terrorism) and ugly (corruption). Too frequently, the good—Iraq's liberation and path toward democratic rule—is not emphasized. Countless American soldiers, sailors, airmen, and marines have complained about the coverage of Iraq by the American media and have argued that such negative coverage ignores the great improvements taking place in Iraq, undermines the support of the American people for the efforts of the military, and aids the insurgency, making the job of the military that much harder. You can find these accounts online, in blogs and other news sources. It takes effort to bypass big media corporations, or, at least, access to the Internet and a bit of time to gain a more accurate impression. But because not everyone has the time, there is a common perception that Iraq is in chaos.

That impression is wholly wrong. Iraq has gone from an authoritarian country to a free country with a constitution. Iraqis are voting in elections for the first time in their lives. More Iraqis participate in the electoral process than Americans. In 90 percent of Iraq, peace and stability reign, and people see the U.S. military as liberators and want to work with the United States as a partner in the region. That is the success of Iraq—and it *is* a success.

To be sure, with economic and political modernization there will be ups and downs. No country has transitioned without profound difficulties from the misrule of a tyrant like Saddam Hussein through liberation to its social and physical reconstruction after generations of horrible abuses and great neglect. But the slope of the curve is positive; Iraq is becoming stronger and more stable every day. Elections are a major indication of progress, and demonstrate that the vast majority of Iraqis support the government. Iraq has about 14 million eligible voters, and 11 million voted in 2005. Its voter participation rate puts the United States to shame. It is common wisdom that the Kurds and Shi'a support the government, but now the majority of Sunnis do as well. For example, voter turnout from the mostly Sunni province of Anbar climbed from 2 percent in the elections of January 30, 2005, when Sunnis where opposed to the government, to 55 percent in the elections of December 2005.

When Iraq is a free and stable country, when its economy flourishes due to its oil wealth, when tourists flock to wonder at the remnants of ancient Babylon, what will those who belittled the Iraqi reconstruction and stabilization efforts say? There will come a day when they have to respond to the facts on the ground and admit that Iraq has been restored to its rightful place in the community of nations and as a leader in the Arab world.

To get to that day, the United States labors to resolve two problems. The first is the insurgency, which is comprised of foreign jihadists who have come to Iraq to fight the United States and the new Iraqi government; criminals who were let loose by Saddam before the invasion in March 2003; and diehard Ba'athists who dream of restoring Saddam Hussein to power and who comprise most of the insurgents. Second, there is the risk of civil war among the three major groups in Iraq: the Shi'a (about 60 percent of Iraq's population), Sunni (between 15 and 20 percent), and Kurds (approximately 17 percent).

The risk of civil war is reduced as long as a large U.S. military force is present in Iraq. Its risk is disappearing as the new Iraqi government finds its strength. The insurgency is a danger the United States confronts now. The insurgency can be defeated and is being defeated by following the classic prescription for doing so—advancing economic, political, and social changes simultaneously with improving the lives of the Iraqi people. Principally, these measures will be done by the Iraqis themselves, not by the United States.

One of the foremost experts on guerrilla warfare, T.E. Lawrence, better known as "Lawrence of Arabia" because he led the Arab guerrilla war against the Ottoman Empire in World War I, famously described fighting an insurgency as "learning how to eat soup with a knife."[3] That is, counterinsurgency operations are messy and they take a long time. The Iraqi and American people and their militaries have to understand both points. Fighting the insurgency in Iraq is messy— at times there is great violence, innocent people are hurt or killed, soldiers are killed brutally, and Iraqi governmental forces are targeted by the insurgents. Both the U.S. and Iraqi forces must have the will power to endure this difficult situation.

Prodigious progress is being made. The infrastructure of Iraq is being rebuilt, and life has returned to normal for the vast majority of Iraqis. But progress takes time, just as eating soup with a knife does. Indeed, time is probably the most important factor for counterinsurgencies. Time is necessary to convince the pro-Saddam diehards in the insurgent movement that Saddam and Ba'ath rule are never coming back—the new Iraq is here to stay. Time is necessary to weaken the insurgency gradually and bring its members to realize that their path is a dead end. The new Iraq is passing them by. Every campaign against guerrilla movements takes time—at least a half a decade, and sometimes several decades. The American and Iraqi people must realize that the counterinsurgency campaign in Iraq will take many years, and they must have the will to stick it out, to persevere through the low points in the campaign against the guerrillas. The insurgency is roughly fixed in size, it is not likely to grow or decline rapidly, and, as history has proven of most insurgencies, they are resilient. Table 3.1 provides important context for the insurgency in Iraq. Historically, major insurgencies averaged a little over thirteen years to resolve.

The United States is undermining guerrillas and destroying their cohesion by demonstrating the integrity and competence of the new government in Iraq—the new government is working for the people of Iraq, all elements of the Iraqi population, and it is an encouraging sign that the Sunni population is participating in the political process.

In contrast, the insurgents want to take the Iraqi people back to the bad old days of torture, executions, and misery under Saddam Hussein and Ba'ath Party rule. The insurgents murder innocent Iraqis and attack Iraqi and Coalition troops but offer no positive vision for the people of Iraq. They can offer only intimidation, subjugation, and hatred. This malicious message resonates less and less with the Iraqi people and with others in the region. Commentators often speak of "the Arab Street," popular opinion in the Arab world, and warn that it will erupt against the United States. The assumption is that the Arab Street will always be opposed to the United States and its allies. The evidence does not support that. In December 2005, the Arab Street did erupt, but it did so against Abu Musab al-Zarqawi. Over two hundred thousand Jordanians protested his terror attacks in Jordan and Iraq. This shows that Arabs, just as everyone else, are fed up with the senseless killing conducted by the insurgents in Iraq.

In order to understand how to defeat the Iraqi insurgency, it is necessary to understand that it does not operate under a central command, but is fractured and comprised of the jihadists, of whom the terrorist Abu Musab al-Zarqawi was the most famous before he was killed by U.S. forces in 2006. These jihadists are religious fanatics and are mostly foreigners. There are also criminals, who are secular and who are using the insurgency to promote criminal aims; and Ba'athists, the members of the failed regime of Saddam Hussein who are secular and hate religious forces.

The jihadists and the Ba'athists are the most dangerous. However, they are divided in both their ideologies and goals. Also, they are only rooted in the Sunni population—and thus they are a minority within a minority. These facts about the insurgency mean that the United States and the Iraqi government have enormous advantages in their struggle against it.

There are five critical steps that must be accomplished by the United States and the Iraqi government to defeat the insurgency; and, indeed, the United States and the Iraqi government are accomplishing all of them. Consequently, the insurgency has great weaknesses and will be defeated over time. But it will take time, as Table 3.1 shows. The American and Iraqi people, as well as the people of allied states like Britain and Australia, have to understand

Table 3.1 Major Insurgencies of the 20th Century

Case	Dates	Duration in Years
Afghanistan	1979–1989	10
Angola UNITA	1975–1991	16
Algeria	1954–1962	8
Arab Revolt	1916–1918	2
Argentina	1970–1976	6
Brazil	1968–1971	3
Chinese Revolution	1927–1949	22
Colombia	1964–2006[a]	42
Cuba I	1898–1902	4
Cuba II	1906–1909	3
Cuba III	1917–1933	16
Cuba IV	1953–1959	6
Cyprus Rebellion	1955–1961	6
Dominican Republic	1916–1924	8
El Salvador	1979–1993	14
Haiti	1915–1934	19
Huk Rebellion	1946–1954	8
Irish Revolution	1916–1921	5
Israel-Palestinian I	1964–1993	29
Israel-Palestinian II	2000–2006[a]	6
Malaya	1947–1960	13
Mau Mau Rebellion	1952–1963	11
Nicaragua	1926–1933	7
Nicaragua (FSLN)	1974–1979	5
Northern Ireland	1969–1998	29
Peru	1980–2006[a]	26
Philippines	1899–1916	17
Portuguese Angola	1961–1975	14
Portuguese East Africa	1961–1975	14
Rif Rebellion	1921–1924	3
Second Boer War	1899–1902	3
Spain ETA	1968–2006[a]	38
Southwest Africa/Namibia	1966–1988	22
Sudan I	1955–1972	17
Sudan II	1983–2005	22
Uruguay	1962–1972	10
Venezuela	1960–1970	10
Vietnam I	1946–1954	8
Vietnam II	1959–1975	16
Average		13.28

[a] Conflict remains ongoing.

this. Based on history, we may expect that the insurgency will last at least thirteen years. Recognizing that it will take time allows Americans and those who wish the new Iraqi government well to steel themselves for a long, low-intensity struggle.

First, joint offensive operations are weakening the insurgency by killing and capturing its members. This is occurring, and the Iraqis are learning much from the U.S. military and intelligence services. The insurgency is fought increasingly by Iraqis rather than Americans. The Iraqis are developing this capability and growing stronger every day.

Second, the Iraqi military and police forces are getting progressively better, and the responsibility for the security of Iraq is being handed off to them from the U.S. military. The United States is building up the Iraqi military and intelligence forces to take over more responsibility from the United States as soon as possible. As the Iraqis grow in strength, the American military forces will be drawn down gradually. A small number of U.S. forces will continue to work with the Iraqis after the bulk of the U.S. military forces have left. They will be assigned directly to Iraqi units in order to train them. In addition, U.S. forces may be expected to provide logistical support as well as heavy armor forces and air support for combat operations.

Intelligence forces are just as important for combating an insurgency as military forces, and there has been much progress in this realm, although it is largely unnoticed by the world's media. At the time of writing, the Iraqis have two intelligence agencies, the Iraqi National Intelligence Service (INIS), to focus on foreign threats such as Iran and Islamic extremists; and the General Security Department (GSD), which is the counterespionage and counterterrorism organization. The INIS and GSD work much like the CIA and FBI in the United States, with one concerned with foreign threats and the other centered on combating espionage and terrorism within the country. The intelligence agencies of the United States, the Iraqi government, and perhaps other allies are infiltrating the insurgency in order to stop it.

Third, the new Iraqi government must root out corruption and work to eliminate local grievances at the grassroots level in order to continue to gain popular support. Additionally, the government has to make economic and political reforms and improvements in the country—from electricity to elections. The good news is that there is great progress on almost every front. The cement holding the guerrillas together has to be destroyed by conveying the message to them and the people that they are holding Iraq back from being the greatest of the Arab countries, as it had been in the past.

Fourth, the new Iraqi government and the U.S. military must maintain the initiative by using guerrilla tactics against the insurgency—reconnaissance, infiltration, hit-and-run tactics, and surprise ambushes to keep the guerrillas off-balance and keep them moving constantly and under threat. This is occurring as well. The safe havens the guerrillas once had in Fallujah and Ramadi are gone now and will not return.

Fifth, the new government has to demonstrate that those in the guerrilla movement will be welcome if they defect. The best way to accomplish this is through an information campaign that proclaims specific cases of people who were guerrillas, or supported them, but who now support the government. In the past, most successful counterinsurgency campaigns have had similar programs. It is in the government's interest to allow the guerrillas to defect to the government's side without fear of repercussions. In fact, the Iraqis have been effective in this regard. Defectors have appeared on Iraqi television to apologize, to state that they were wrong to engage in terrorism, and to appeal to their former comrades to end their terrorism and join the government.

The United States will be successful in Iraq, and the insurgency will wither away, despite the best efforts of Iran to keep it going. But Americans must understand that an independent and free Iraq will not be a toady or pawn of the United States. The United States may expect to have significant differences with a free Iraq, and this may cause frustration in Washington. When Iraq's interests coincide with those of the United States, Washington may expect to be able to work closely with Baghdad. In other words, we may expect Iraq not to be subservient to the United States, but an ally of it: a major reason for America to have fought to liberate Iraq from tyranny.

Most poignantly, in 2006, U.S. Army Colonel H.R. McMaster, who was a hero in Operation Desert Storm, reflected on his long experience in Iraq as commander of the Third Armored Cavalry Regiment and what he could communicate to the American people to permit them to understand the conditions in Iraq:

> I was patrolling after an attack on police recruits. It was a suicide attack immediately after the operation. And I was walking with a small element up the street of Hasan Koy, which previously was a hostile area. I saw an Iraqi coming toward me on crutches, a young man, and I thought, well, this is an insurgent, a terrorist….So I went up to him and started asking him some questions. It turns out he was wounded in that attack where he was waiting in line to be recruited for the Iraqi police. He was now walking on crutches across town to join the Iraqi army so he could defeat these terrorists and bring security to his family.
>
> I guess what people don't get to see is, they don't get to see how resolute and how determined these courageous Iraqis are. And the other thing I wish we could communicate more clearly is the relationships we've developed with people. I mean, we've made lifetime friends among the good Iraqi people. So the Iraqi people you tend to see most on coverage…are the ones…who are conducting attacks against us….But there are so many good people in this country who deserve security and who

are doing everything they can to build a future for their families, their towns and their country.[4]

A major step in remaking the Middle East began with Operation Iraqi Freedom. As a result of the success of Operation Iraqi Freedom, the United States has been able to foster change in the region from Lebanon to Iraq. The change has been along the following parameters. First, regimes opposed to the interests of the United States are pressured to reform or face the possibility of being removed. Second, the United States should spread democracy in the Middle East if this can be accomplished without hurting existing friendly regimes.[5] This is part of a larger effort to promote liberal democracy around the world. The more liberal democracies there are in the world, the more congenial for the United States and the easier it is for the United States to maintain its hegemony.

However, I am a good realist, so if there is a tension between democracy and maintaining a pro-American government, then the latter is the right choice for the United States at this time. American decision-makers should keep in mind the Shah of Iran, a U.S. ally, who was undermined by President Carter, when he pushed too hard and too quickly, for democratic reform. The Shah fell and was replaced by a much worse government—the rule of Ayatollah Khomeini. Thirty years later, the United States still grapples with the consequences. Accordingly, what is vitally important is that governments are supportive and respectful of the interests of the United States. Fundamentally, realism should govern the foreign policy of the United States—America's interests first.

Primacy Is the Right Grand Strategy for the United States

There is no viable alternative grand strategy for the United States than primacy. Primacy is the best and most effective means to maintain the security and safety of the United States for the reasons I argued in chapter 1. However, it is also the best because every other grand strategic "alternative" is a chimera and can only weaken the United States, threaten the security and safety of the American people, and introduce great peril for the United States and for other countries.

A large part of what makes primacy such a success is that other countries know where the United States stands, what it will defend, and that it will be involved in disputes, both great and small. Accordingly, other countries have to respect the interests of the United States or face the consequences. Offshore balancing incurs the risks of primacy without its benefits. It pledges that the United States will defend its interests with air power and sea power, but not land power. That is curious because we could defend our interests with land power but choose not to, suggesting our threat to defend is not serious, which weakens our credibility and invites challenges to the interests of the United

States. Offshore balancing increases the probability of conflict for the United States. It raises the danger that the interests of the United States will be challenged not only from foes like China and Iran, but, perversely, also from countries now allied with the United States like Japan and Turkey.

General Douglas MacArthur said that there was no substitute for victory. Just as there is no substitute for victory, there is no alternative for leadership. For if the United States does not provide that leadership to its allies by pledging to use all of its power in their defense, then they will provide their own security. If the United States does not lead the world, another hegemon will rise to replace it. That hegemon will be China. China will then be in a position to dictate to the rest of world, including the United States. The United States would be far less secure in such a world.

This is because, first, the physical security of the United States would be jeopardized. Due to its military superiority, China would have the ability to triumph over the United States in the event of war or an international crisis, like the 1962 Cuban Missile Crisis. The United States would be forced to back down, thus placing China's interests before its own. China would be able to blackmail the United States, to coerce it to do Beijing's bidding. The United States would be relegated to the role of pawn on the international chessboard.

Second, the United States would lose its allies and global influence. As China's power grew, countries would look to Beijing to be their ally in order to gain security and assistance. It will be the case that countries long allied with the United States, such as Australia, will no longer be allies as their interests require them to look to Beijing and away from Washington.

Third, the Chinese economy will dominate the global economy. Worldwide, both countries and businesses will look to China not simply as a market, as they do now, but the economic locomotive of the world's economy, as the lender of last resort, and as the stabilizer of economic exchange and the international trade and monetary regimes. Countries will have to appease China economically or face the consequences of its wrath.

Fourth, Chinese will be the language of diplomacy, trade and commerce, transportation and navigation, the Internet, world sport, and global culture. Additionally, China will dominate science and technology, in all of its forms—the life sciences, bioengineering, computer science, and even space exploration. It will be a great blow to the pride of the United States, greater than Sputnik in 1957, when China travels to the Moon, as they plan to do, and plants the communist flag on Mars, and perhaps other planets in the future.

In sum, the United States will be far less influential and subjected to the role that China, not decision-makers in Washington or the American people, wants it to play. Fundamentally, the security of the United States would be dependent on the decisions made in China. That is the world of the future if the United States does not maintain its primacy.

To abandon its leadership role would be a fundamental mistake of American grand strategy. Indeed, in the great history of the United States, there is no parallel, no previous case, where the United States has made such a titanic grand strategic blunder. It would surpass by far its great mistake of 1812, when the young and ambitious country gambled and declared war against a mighty empire, the British, believing London was too distracted by the tremendous events on the Continent—the formidable military genius of Napoleon and the prodigious threat from the French empire and its allies—to notice while it conquered Canada.

The citizens of the United States cannot pretend that, by weakening ourselves, other countries will be nice and respect its security and interests. To suggest this implies a naïveté and innocence about international politics that would be charming, if only the consequences of such an opinion were not so serious. Throughout its history, the United States has never refrained from acting boldly to secure its interests. It should not be timid now.

Many times in the great history of the United States, the country faced difficult decisions—decisions of confrontation or appeasement—and significant threats—the British, French, Spanish, Germans, Italians, Japanese, and Soviets. It always has recognized those threats and faced them down, to emerge victorious. The United States should have the confidence to do so now against China not simply because to do so maximizes its power and security or ensures it is the dominant voice in the world's affairs, but because it is the last, best hope of humanity.

The United States faces a choice as significant as any in its history: To maintain leadership or to live in a world dominated by the Communist Chinese, the last significant representative of a cruel and failed ideology. A world dominated by the United States, the country Walt Whitman called "essentially the greatest poem," is far superior for the whole of the world's population than a world controlled by the Communist Chinese.[6] In this book and in academic settings, we may debate the issues that concern that choice. Intellectually, that is entirely appropriate. But emotionally and instinctually, each of us knows that, should any country be dominant, the United States is the best choice to exercise such power. That recognition alone quite perfectly answers the debate over the American Empire.

Notes

1. The greatest support for offensive realist behavior comes from human evolution. Its expectation of human behaviors is precisely what would be necessary to survive in the human past and is supported by empirical evidence from tribal societies, archaeology, and the behaviors of other animals as documented by ethologists. See Bradley A. Thayer, *Darwin and International Relations: On the Evolutionary Origins of War and Ethnic Conflict* (Lexington: University Press of Kentucky, 2004).
2. *The Oxford Dictionary of Quotations*, 5th ed. (New York: Oxford University Press, 1999), p. 566.

3. T.E. Lawrence, *The Seven Pillars of Wisdom: A Triumph* (New York: Anchor Books, 1991), p. 193.
4. U.S. Department of Defense, "News Briefing with Col. H.R. McMaster," transcript, January 27, 2006, available at: http://defenselink.mil/transcripts/2006/tr20060127-12385.html.
5. A thoughtful assessment concerning the ability of the United States to advance democracy in the Middle East is provided by Noah Feldman, *After Jihad: America and the Struggle for Islamic Democracy* (New York: Farrar, Straus and Giroux, 2003).
6. Walt Whitman, "Preface to *Leaves of Grass*," in Mark Van Doren, ed., *The Portable Walt Whitman* (New York: Penguin Books, 1973), p. 5.

4

Reply to Bradley Thayer
The Illusion of the American Empire

CHRISTOPHER LAYNE

Introduction

In this chapter, I focus on the costs of the American Empire. Contrary to its proponents' claims, the strategy of primacy and empire comes with a steep price tag. It is increasingly clear that the United States will be hard-pressed to afford the costs of empire without undermining its economy. Moreover, in addition to its economic impact, the strategy of primacy and empire has a corrosive effect on democracy in the United States and is at odds with America's most cherished political values.

The Costs of Empire

Economics and Empire

At the end of the day, Americans must ask not only if the strategy of primacy and empire makes America more secure, or more *in*secure, but also ask what are that strategy's costs, and can America afford them? It is, of course, a truism that economic strength is the foundation of American primacy. A strong economy generates the wealth that pays for the extensive military apparatus necessary to maintain America's dominant geopolitical position. But here the United States confronts a problem that traditionally has perplexed the statesman of great powers: striking the proper balance between public and private investment in the domestic economy, domestic consumption, and investment in military power. On the one hand, because they are expected to provide welfare as well as national security, modern states constantly face the dilemma of allocating scarce resources among the competing external and domestic policies. At the same time, grand strategists must be cognizant of the danger that overinvesting in security in the short term can weaken the state in the long term by eroding the economic foundations of national power.[1] Finding

121

the right balance between security and economic stability is a timeless grand strategic conundrum.[2]

Paul Kennedy's 1987 book, *The Rise and Fall of the Great Powers*, ignited an important debate about the sustainability of American primacy. In a nutshell, Kennedy argued that the United States was doomed to repeat a familiar pattern of imperial decline because the excessive costs of military commitments abroad was eroding the economic foundations of American power. An important backdrop to Kennedy's book was the so-called twin deficits: endless federal budget deficits, and a persistent balance of trade deficit. As a result, the United States had quickly gone from being the leading creditor state in the international economic system to being the leading debtor and had became dependent on inflows of foreign—especially Japanese—capital. As Robert Gilpin noted (also in 1987), the inflow of Japanese capital "supported the dollar, helped finance the [Reagan] defense buildup, and contributed to American prosperity. More importantly, it masked the relative economic decline of the United States."[3] The late 1980s debate about possible American decline was terminated abruptly, however; first, by the Soviet Union's collapse, and then by U.S. economic revival during the Clinton administration, which also saw the yearly federal budget deficits give way to annual budget surpluses.

The proponents of American primacy and empire assert both that the United States can afford this grand strategy and that American economy is fundamentally robust. These claims might come as news to most Americans, however. When a company like General Motors—historically one of the flagship corporations of the U.S. economy—teeters on the edge of bankruptcy and sheds some 126,000 jobs—rosy descriptions about the strength of the U.S. economy ring hollow.[4] Similarly, the notion that the U.S. economy is healthy certainly would not be shared by the hundreds of thousands of U.S. workers who have lost their jobs in America's ever-contracting manufacturing sector—often because their jobs have been outsourced to China or India. Even more worrisome, future outsourcing of American jobs is not likely to be confined just to blue-collar workers. Rather, an increasing number of high-skill/high-education jobs will flow from the United States to other countries.[5] Another warning sign that all is not well with the U.S. economy is the "middle class squeeze"—the fact that middle class incomes in the United States have been stagnant since the early 1970s. Doubtless, the American economy has made gains in productivity, but those gains are being enjoyed by only a small number of Americans in the highest income brackets. As the *Financial Times* recently noted:

> Since 1973, the income of the top 10 per cent of American earners has grown by 111 per cent, while the income of the middle fifth has grown by only 15 per cent. That trend has become more pronounced in the

last few years. Between 1998 and 2004, the median income of American households fell by 3.8 per cent.[6]

To some the American economy may seem buoyant, but the hollowing-out of America's manufacturing industrial base, the outsourcing of American jobs, and stagnant middle-class incomes are flashing red lights warning that all is far from well with the U.S. economy.

Indeed, the economic vulnerabilities that Kennedy pinpointed in the late 1980s may have receded into the background during the 1990s, but they did not disappear. Once again, the United States is running endless federal budget deficits, and the trade deficit has grown worse and worse. The United States still depends on capital inflows from abroad, with China fast replacing Japan as America's most important creditor, to finance its deficit spending, finance private consumption, and maintain the dollar's position as the international economic system's reserve currency. Because of the twin deficits, the underlying fundamentals of the U.S. economy are out of alignment. The United States cannot continue to live beyond its means indefinitely. Sooner or later, the bill will come due in the form of sharply higher taxes and interest rates—and, consequently, economic slowdown. And, as the United States borrows more and more to finance its budget and trade deficits, private investment is likely to be "crowded out" of the marketplace, with predictable effects on the economy's long-term health. In a word (or two), the United States is suffering from "fiscal overstretch."[7]

Economically, the United States is looking at the same problems in the early twenty-first century that it faced in the 1980s (and which had been building since the early 1960s). Except this time, the long-term prognosis is bleaker, because there are two big differences between now and then.[8] First, during the Cold War, Japan (and, during the 1970s, West Germany) subsidized U.S. budget and trade deficits as a *quid pro quo* for American security guarantees. It will be interesting to see whether an emerging geopolitical rival like China—or, for that matter, the European Union—will be as willing to underwrite American primacy in coming decades. Second, there have been big changes on the economic side of the ledger that cast a long shadow over America's long-term economic prospects. For one thing, the willingness of other states to cover America's debts no longer can be taken for granted. Already, key central banks are signaling their lack of confidence in the dollar by diversifying their currency holdings.[9] There are rumblings, too, that OPEC may start pricing oil in euros and that the dollar could be supplanted by the euro as the international economy's reserve currency. Should this happen, the United States no longer could afford to maintain its primacy.[10]

The domestic economic picture is not so promising, either. The annual federal budget deficits are just the tip of the iceberg. The real problems are the federal government's huge unfunded liabilities for entitlement programs that will begin to come due about a decade hence.[11] Moreover, defense spending and entitlement expenditures are squeezing out discretionary spending on domestic programs. Just down the road, the United States is facing stark "warfare" or "welfare" choices between, on the one hand, maintaining the overwhelming military capabilities upon which its primacy rests, or, on the other hand, discretionary spending on domestic needs and funding Medicare, Medicaid, and Social Security.[12] Here, the proponents of primacy and empire overlook a huge change in the U.S. fiscal picture. They assert that the United States can afford its imperial strategy because defense spending now accounts only for about 4 percent of U.S. gross domestic product (GDP), which is well below Cold War levels. This is true, but very misleading.

Why? Because under the Bush II administration, the norm in the allocation of federal discretionary spending that prevailed throughout most of the Clinton administration has been reversed: the Pentagon's share of discretionary spending in the federal budget once again exceeds domestic spending. What really matters is not the percentage of GDP absorbed by defense spending, but the Defense Department's share of discretionary federal spending. Coupled with mandatory spending on entitlements (and debt service), defense spending is squeezing discretionary federal spending on domestic programs. Given the long-term unsustainability of federal budget deficits, coming years will see strong pressures to reduce federal spending. However, because defense, entitlements, and debt service together account for 80 percent of federal spending, it is obvious that—as long as U.S. defense spending continues at the high levels mandated by the strategy of primacy and empire—the burden of federal deficit reduction will fall primarily on the remaining 20 percent of the budget—that is, on discretionary domestic spending. In plain English, that means that the United States will be spending more on guns and less and less on butter—"butter" in this case meaning, among other things, federal government investments in education, infrastructure, and research, which all are crucial to keeping the United States competitive in the international economy. Sooner rather than later, Americans will be compelled to ask whether spending on the American Empire is more important than spending on domestic needs here at home.[13]

In fact, if anything, the costs of the American Empire are likely to increase in coming years. There are two reasons for this. First, there is the spiraling cost of the Iraq quagmire. As some readers may recall, the Bush II administration's economic advisor, Lawrence Lindsey, was fired because he dared to predict that the cost of the Iraq war, and its aftermath, might reach $200 billion. The administration predicted that the war itself would cost no more than $50–$60 billion and that Iraq would pay for its own postwar recovery from oil sales. Of course, the United States to date has borne most of the cost of Iraq's postwar recovery. As far as the ultimate economic costs of the war are concerned, it is apparent that the administration's $50–$60 billion estimate was a projection right out of Fantasyland. Recently, Joesph Sitglitz (a Nobel laureate in economics) and Linda Bilmes have indicated that, at the end of the day, the budgetary cost of the war will be somewhere between $750 billion and $1,184 billion (which includes, among other things, the costs of military operations, Veterans Administration costs attributable to the war, increased defense spending, and additional interest on the national debt). Moreover, they estimate that the direct and indirect costs of the war to the U.S. economy will be between $1,026 billion and $1,854 billion.[14]

The second reason that defense spending is likely to increase is the simple fact that the U.S. military is not large enough to meet all of America's imperial commitments. Since the Cold War's end, the United States has shown every sign of succumbing to the "hegemon's temptation"—the temptation to use its military power promiscuously—and Iraq, along with the simultaneous crises with Iran and North Korea, have highlighted the mismatch between America's hegemonic ambitions and the military resources available to support them. To maintain its dominance, the American military will have to be expanded in size, because it is too small to meet present—and likely future—commitments.[15] No one can say for certain how long significant U.S. forces will need to remain in Iraq (and Afghanistan), but it's safe to say that substantial numbers of troops will be there for a long time. At the same time, in addition to the ongoing War on Terrorism (and the concomitant requirements of homeland defense), the United States faces possible future conflicts with North Korea, Iran, and China.

During the past fifteen years or so since the Soviet Union's collapse, the United States was able to postpone the need to grapple with the painful issues Kennedy raised in 1987. However, the chickens are coming home to roost, and those questions soon will have to be faced. Gilpin's 1987 description of America's grand strategic and economic dilemmas is, if anything, even more timely today:

> With a decreased rate of economic growth and a low rate of national savings, the United States was living and defending commitments far beyond its means. In order to bring its commitments and power back into balance once again, the United States would one day have to cut back further on its overseas commitments, reduce the American standard of living, or decrease domestic productive investment even more than it already had. In the meantime, American hegemony was threatened by a potentially devastating fiscal crisis.[16]

At some point, the relative decline of U.S. economic power that is in the offing will bring American primacy to an end. In the shorter term, however, the United States can prolong its primacy *if* Americans are willing to pay the price in terms of higher taxes, reduced consumption, and curtailment of domestic programs. But, of course, there is a treadmill-like aspect to preserving the

American Empire, because perpetuating it will hasten the weakening of the economic base upon which it rests.

The Domestic Political Consequences of Empire

In the most memorable—and controversial—passage of his second Inaugural Address, President George W. Bush declared that, "We are led, by events and common sense, to one conclusion: The survival of liberty in our land increasingly depends on the success of liberty in other lands. The best hope for peace in our world is the expansion of freedom in all the world. America's vital interests and deepest beliefs are now one." In claiming that the survival of democracy in America depends on the successful export of democracy abroad, Bush has reprised Wilsonianism's most dubious thesis. Like his predecessors—going back to Woodrow Wilson himself—Bush believes that America can avoid becoming a "garrison state" only by following a policy of strategic internationalism and democracy promotion abroad. Contrary to Bush's assertion in his Inaugural Address, however, an imperial foreign policy is antithetical to the flourishing of democracy and liberty here in the United States.

It may be true that America's Founding Fathers envisioned that the United States would become an "empire of liberty," but it is also true that their vision of empire was confined to North America. Moreover, they were crystal clear that their vision of empire was based on important values rooted in America's own history and political culture, including a republican form of government, protection of individual liberties, and suspicion of state power. They also understood full well that if the United States ever got mixed up in the kind of overseas imperialism practiced by the European great powers, these American values would be imperiled. This argument was reprised during the post–Spanish–American War great debate of 1898–99 about whether the United States should annex the Philippines. In his classic anti-imperialist essay, "The Conquest of the United States by Spain," William Graham Sumner predicted—accurately—that if the United States went into the empire business, its unique political culture would be transformed and its system of government would come to resemble those of the other great imperial powers of the day: Britain, France, Germany, and Russia. In more recent times, *real* conservatives like Dwight Eisenhower and Robert Taft—a very different breed from the *faux* conservative neocon cheerleaders for American Empire—warned that the Cold War was effectuating a domestic transformation of the United States and that the core values of limited government, shared congressional and executive responsibility for foreign policy, and fiscal prudence were being eroded.

Bush's words about defending liberty and freedom by promoting it abroad ring hollow. Seldom in American history has an administration displayed less regard for the Constitution, the law—domestic and international—and civil liberties. The truth is that by—purportedly—promoting democracy abroad, the Bush administration is trampling upon it at home. To start with, contrary to all settled Constitutional principles, the administration has claimed that the president's war powers are all but unconstrained. In essence, the administration claims that as long as it is in the pursuit of "national security," the president can do pretty much whatever he deems necessary. The result of this sweeping assertion of power can be seen in the administration's use of the National Security Agency (NSA) to engage in domestic surveillance of phone calls and emails. As James Risen has written, since 9/11, "The Bush administration has swept aside nearly thirty years of rules and regulations and has secretly brought the NSA back into the business of domestic espionage."[17] As Risen reports, shortly after 9/11 Bush signed an executive order authorizing the NSA to monitor and eavesdrop on virtually all telephone calls and email traffic inside the United States. The executive order was a deliberate end run around the Foreign Intelligence Surveillance Act, which requires the NSA to obtain a court order before eavesdropping on domestic communications. Under Bush's order, the NSA is completely unaccountable; there is no judicial—or other—oversight of its domestic surveillance. As Risen notes, "the NSA determines, on its own, which telephone numbers and e-mail addresses to monitor. The NSA doesn't have to get approval from the White House, the Justice Department, or anyone else in the Bush administration before it begins eavesdropping on a specific phone line inside the United States."[18]

The Patriot Act is another instance where the Bush administration has used 9/11 to roll back civil liberties. Under the Patriot Act, the administration is using "national security letters," which allow secret surveillance and information gathering of "U.S. residents and visitors who are not alleged to be terrorists or spies."[19] As the *Washington Post* reported, "Issued by FBI field supervisors, national security letters do not need the imprimatur of a prosecutor, grand jury or judge."[20] Moreover, the Patriot Act prohibits the target of a national security letter from disclosing to "any person" that they have been served with such a letter. On its face, the language prohibits a person, or organization, that is served with a national security letter from contacting a lawyer and challenging the letter's legality.[21] The FBI uses national security letters to obtain the very kinds of information about citizens' lives that historically has been protected by the Fourth Amendment's proscription against unreasonable searches and seizures, including phone records, correspondence, financial information, and even the books a citizen checks out from the library, or the movies a citizen rents from a video store. Real conservatives know that when the government is given such unchecked, wide-ranging powers to intrude into the lives of citizens, civil liberties are at risk. As Bob Barr, a conservative former congressman has said, "The beef with the NSLs is that they don't have even a pretense of judicial or impartial scrutiny. There's no checks and balances whatever on them. It is simply some bureaucrat's decision that they want information, and they can basically just go and get it." This, apparently, is the Bush administration's version of democracy in America.

The Bush administration's treatment of "enemy combatants" taken prisoner as part of the so-called Global War on Terror is another example of how the administration has acted contrary to America's deepest values. Asserting a dubious legal claim that it can seize enemy combatants and bring them before military tribunals, the administration has set up internment facilities at Guantanamo Bay, Cuba, the Abu Ghraib prison in Iraq, and the Bagram air base in Afghanistan. The detainees in these camps are—so the administration claims—entirely outside the jurisdiction of the U.S. legal system (and outside the purview of the Geneva Conventions on the treatment of prisoners of war). According to the administration, the United States can keep enemy combatants—even American citizens suspected of engaging in terrorist acts—in custody indefinitely and is not required to charge them with a crime, afford them legal counsel, or even bring them to trial.

Shielded from judicial oversight, the administration has deliberately promulgated policies that have shaded applicable international law to allow U.S. interrogators to engage in the torture "lite" of enemy combatants at Guantanamo Bay. The administration also has authorized the use of hard-core torture by allowing the CIA to establish secret prisons abroad, and to carry out a policy of so-called renditions (where the United States hands over enemy combatants to countries where interrogation techniques are not limited by legal niceties).[22] Although the overwhelming consensus among experts is that torture invariably fails to produce useful information—that is, it is not cost effective—the United States has paid a huge price in terms of its international standing for its treatment of enemy combatants. As Stephen Walt observes, "imagine how America's image might have been improved had it placed the prisoners at Guantanamo Bay under the protections of the Geneva Convention and had Secretary of Defense Rumsfeld apologized and resigned in response to the torture scandal at Abu Ghraib prison."[23] While these policies would not, Walt admits, eliminate all the manifestations of anti-Americanism abroad, they "would have made it much harder to portray the United States as a 'rogue superpower,' and it would have given America's friends around the world far more effective ammunition in the battle for world opinion."[24] Not only have the administration's detention and torture policies sullied America's reputation abroad, but in a practical sense those policies are counterproductive.[25] Abu Ghraib, for example, injected new life into the Iraqi insurgency and was a veritable recruiting poster for Islamic terrorist groups. Most of all, however, the Bush administration's policies with respect to enemy combatants have inflicted a deep wound to America's own self-image as a decent and humane nation. As the British learned in India and Ireland, and the French in Algeria, imperial policies and democratic values don't mix.

Bush's words about liberty and freedom ring hollow in another sense, too. American officials want to promote democracy abroad, but are loathe to practice it in the conduct of U.S. foreign policy. The reason that democracies—

like the United States—are *supposed* to be peaceful is that citizens can hold accountable leaders who squander lives and treasure on unnecessary wars. Moreover, democracy is *supposed* to ensure that policy making is transparent, and policies are subject to open debate. That's the theory, at any rate. But it's based on a romantic notion of how American democracy works that even a sophisticated fourth grader knows is illusory.

What this theory leaves out is what political scientists call "the state"—a nation's central decision-makers and the institutional mechanisms through which they exercise power. Because it is overtly antistatist, liberal political theory downplays the role of the state. But even in liberal countries like the United States, the state is an autonomous actor. That is, rather than by being constrained by civil society, the state mobilizes the levers of power to manipulate civil society and harness it to support state policies. For example, to maintain public support for an imperial policy abroad—and their grip on political power at home—American foreign policy elites have since the early 20th century engaged in a calculated policy of threat exaggeration to overcome the stubborn fact that, because of geography and its overwhelming power, the United States is basically immune from serious threats from abroad. Consequently, for well over a century, official American rhetoric has been based on a finely honed set of images: dangerous ideologies, a "shrinking world," and falling dominoes. To mobilize support for their policies, the American foreign policy elite has created a rhetorical climate of fear in order to convince Americans that only strategic internationalism can preserve the nation's security and way of life.

Another way the state manipulates civil society is by controlling the flow of information and shaping public opinion. In the U.S. government, there even is a name for this: "perception management." Of course, perception management simply is a fancy term for sophisticated lying. It is the kind of manipulation of the truth that the Bush administration engaged in during the run-up to the Iraq war—the claim that Iraq had weapons of mass destruction and—even more—the assertion that Saddam Hussein was linked to the 9/11 attacks. As Louis Fisher rightly observes, the decision to go to war with Iraq "cast a dark shadow over the health of U.S. political institutions and the celebrated system of democratic debate and checks and balances."[26] It's not just the Bush II administration that has engaged in perception management, however. It is a bipartisan tool. During the Kosovo war, the Clinton administration justified U.S. intervention by implying that Serbia was engaged in, as Defense Secretary William Cohen said, "a horrific slaughter"—a genocide of Holocaust-like proportions against the Kosovars. After the war, these claims were found to be wholly without foundation.

In the long term, the actual facts may come to light. They did with respect to this administration's false claims about Iraq and with the Clinton administration's wild exaggerations about Kosovo. But in the short term, perception management allows policy-makers to stifle dissent, preempt congressional opposition, and gain a free hand to carry out their interventions. By the time the congress, the public, and the media realize they were misled, it's too late, because the official policy already has been implemented and is irreversible. Indeed, some policy-makers have been quite candid in urging the need for the United States to formulate military strategies that will enable it to intervene and prevail quickly before congressional or public opposition can mobilize. In an interview with the *International Herald Tribune* on the eve of his retirement as NATO Supreme Commander, Wesley K. Clark urged precisely that the United States adopt strategies that could design around the constraining effects of the democratic process.

It's quite evident that the Bush administration has a rather blinkered view of the democratic process. On the eve of his second inauguration, Bush claimed that the November 2004 election had "legitimized" his foreign policy. In a 2005 *New Yorker* article, Seymour Hersh showed that this is exactly what top administration policy-makers believe.[27] That is, they believe that in the 2004 presidential election, the American electorate gave the administration a second-term green light to go after "outposts of tyranny" like Iran, Syria, and North Korea. Just how an electoral victory procured through deceit and disinformation—and by equating disagreement with the administration's foreign policy with a lack of patriotism—amounts to a mandate is an interesting question. Still, as Bush himself put it, November 2004 was the administration's "accountability *moment*." This is a curious view of the American political process. In the United States, the accountability of officials is supposed to be ongoing, not momentary.

If the administration puts its current plans into effect, soon we may be denied even momentary accountability in matters of war and peace. The *New York Times*, the *Washington Post*, and the *New Yorker* have all reported that the administration is moving to gut the Central Intelligence Agency and transfer key responsibilities for intelligence gathering and covert operations to the Pentagon—where these activities will be shielded from outside oversight and accountability. That is, the Bush administration is trying to restructure the national security apparatus so that it can wage "low-intensity wars" in secret. So much for the notion that, in a democracy, policy is supposed to be made openly so its merits can be debated fully. And so much for the notion that policy-makers are to be held accountable for their actions.

The American Empire has been bad news for democracy and civil liberties in America. Under the Bush II administration, Americans have seen the very apotheosis of Empire: a government that has built its Iraq policy on a foundation of lies and the doctoring of intelligence, made an unprecedentedly sweeping assertion of presidential war powers, and has rolled back civil liberties. Moreover, the administration has attempted to place its actions beyond the realm of congressional and public scrutiny. All of this is corrosive of American democracy. As Louis Fisher observes:

> Democracy depends on laws but much more on trust. Constitutions and statutes are necessarily general in scope, placing a premium on judgment and discretion. Without confidence in what public officials say and do, laws are easily twisted to satisfy private ends. Leaders who claim to act in the national interest may, instead, pursue personal or partisan agendas....In an age of terrorism, especially after 9/11, the public needs full trust in the integrity of its elected leaders and in the intelligence agencies that guide crucial decisions. For all the sophistication of the U.S. political and economic system, if trust is absent, so is popular control.[28]

Under the Bush administration, the pursuit of American Empire indeed has weakened trust in government. Americans need to reassert their control in order to preserve a vibrant democracy here in the United States. The Bush administration has disregarded Dwight Eisenhower's sage warning that, "We are defending a way of life and must be respectful of it...not only so as not to violate its principles and precepts, but also not to destroy from within what we are trying to defend from without." This is what *real* conservatism is all about. Americans should not countenance the administration's assault on the Constitution and on America's values and reputation for fairness and decency. They should demand that the Bush administration abandon its imperial policy of "democracy promotion" abroad and, instead, turn its focus to practicing democracy here in the United States.

Beyond Primacy and Empire: Toward a New Grand Strategy

America's greatest foreign policy realist thinkers—Hans Morgenthau, George F. Kennan, Walter Lippmann, Robert W. Tucker, and Kenneth Waltz—have always understood that power has both a seductive and corrupting effect on those who wield it—even the United States: "The possession of great power has often tempted nations to the unnecessary and foolish employment of force, vices from which we are not immune."[29] Similarly, they also have been rightly concerned that a *too* powerful America would instill feelings of fear and insecurity among the other states in the international system. Kenneth Waltz has stressed the dangers that ensue whenever power becomes too tightly concentrated (whether internationally or domestically). As he has put it, "I distrust hegemonic power, whoever may wield it, because it is so easily misused."[30] Here, Waltz paralleled Edmund Burke's famous—and very timely—injunction about the boomerang effects that follow when overwhelming power is married to overweening ambition:

> Among precautions against ambition, it may not be amiss to take one precaution against our *own*. I must fairly say, I dread *our* own power and our *own* ambition; I dread our being too much dreaded....It is ridiculous to say we are not men, and that, as men we shall never wish to aggrandize ourselves in some way or other...we may say that we shall not abuse this astonishing and hitherto unheard of power. But every other nation will think we shall abuse it. It is impossible but that, sooner or later, this state of things must produce a combination against us which may end in our ruin.[31]

Burke's warning resonates today, because as the diplomatic historian Walter LaFeber observes, "In the post–September 11 world, exceptionalism, combined with the immensity of American power, hinted at the dangers of a nation so strong that others could not check it, and so self-righteous that it could not check itself."[32]

Realists understand that notions of American exceptionalism can warp U.S. grand strategy. Waltz—echoing Morgenthau's injunction that the task of realism is to prevent statesmen from "moral excess and political folly"—has recognized that an America ensconced in a position of global primacy would be tempted to equate its own preferences with justice and be just as likely as other powerful states to use its power unwisely: "One cannot assume that the leaders of a nation superior in power will always define policies with wisdom, devise tactics with finite calculation, and apply force with forbearance."[33] It is for this reason that realists like Lippmann, Kennan, Morgenthau, and Waltz have highlighted the dangers that await if the United States gives in to the temptations of primacy and have counseled instead that the United States pursue a grand strategy based on prudence and self-restraint.

Realists always have held that grand strategy must be grounded in the concept of national interest. They also have known, however, that the very term "national interest" invariably has a moral—or normative—dimension. This is because there is no single, objectively "true" national interest.[34] Rather, the concept of "national interest describes a starting point, an approach to formulating policy."[35] Thinking in terms of national interest improves the quality of statecraft by forcing decision-makers to ask the right questions—about the relation of ends to means, about what is necessary versus what merely is desirable—when they formulate grand strategy. Applied to grand strategy, the concept of national interest reminds policy-makers that they must be guided by what the sociologist Max Weber called the "ethic of responsibility"—which, in layman's terms, restates the familiar injunction that the road to hell is paved with good intentions—and, hence, that decision-makers must "be calculators instead of crusaders."[36] Primacy and empire, however, serve to infuse American grand strategy with precisely the crusading mentality and self-righteousness that the United States should want to avoid.

For the last century, U.S. policy-makers have been haunted by the fear that the closure of other regions of the world to the penetration of America's Wilsonian ideology will destroy "the American way of life." As the diplomatic historian Frank Ninkovich has put it, U.S. foreign policymakers have believed (and still do) that closure of these regions would "cut off the oxygen without which American society, and liberal institutions generally, would asphyxiate."[37] Wilsonianism always has been based on the fear that unless the United States can remake the world in its own ideological image, it will be transformed at home into a "garrison state." That is, unless American ideology is preeminent globally, the United States might have to accept curtailed political liberties and economic regimentation at home in order to ensure its security in an ideologically hostile world. This is why U.S. foreign policy rests on the assumption that political and economic liberalism cannot flourish at home unless they are safe abroad.

This worldview is the outgrowth of a fundamental pathology in American liberalism. As Louis Hartz pointed out in his classic book, *The Liberal Tradition in America*, in domestic politics, American liberalism has been deeply hostile to alternative ideologies and preemptively has sought to suppress them. American liberalism can be secure at home—or so it is believed—only when it has no rivals. Not to put too fine a point on it, American liberalism—supposedly an ideology of tolerance—aims to extirpate other ideologies and worldviews. Wilsonianism seeks to replicate externally American liberalism's domestic primacy. In other words, American liberal ideology is the fountainhead of the American Empire.

Long before Saddam Hussein came down the pike, "regime change" has been a favored tool of American foreign policy. Here, however, U.S. grand strategy tends to become a self-fulfilling prophecy, because it causes states that might not otherwise have done so to become threats. That is, Wilsonianism causes the United States to be more, not less, insecure than it would be if its external ambitions were more modest. When, by asserting the universal applicability of its own ideology, the United States challenges the legitimacy of other regimes—by labeling them as outposts of tyranny or members of an axis of evil—the effect is to increase those states' sense of isolation and vulnerability. With good reason, such states fear that their survival could be at risk. Iran is a good example. Given that states—and regimes—are highly motivated to survive, it's no surprise that others respond to American policy by adopting strategies that give them a chance to do so—like acquiring WMD capabilities and supporting terrorism. One thing is for sure: because of its Wilsonian foundations, the American Empire is a recipe for confrontation and antagonism with "others."

Wilsonianism views the world as sharply divided between good states and bad—or even "evil"—states. And the policy implications are obvious: if bad states are the source of war and terrorism, the prescription is for the

United States to use its power and transform them into good states. In this respect, Wilsonianism reveals the dark side of American ideology: permanent (or semipermanent) war, and—ironically—the transformation of the United States into the very garrison state—or, as it came to be known during the Cold War, "national security state"—that the strategy of primacy and empire was supposed to prevent. America's *real* realists—Kennan, Lippmann, Morgenthau, Tucker, and Waltz—have always feared that the pursuit of primacy would lead to excessive interventionism and cause the United States to adopt both a crusading mentality and a spirit of intolerance. Moreover, the real realists have understood that the United States pays a big price at home for overreaching abroad. For real realists, foreign policy restraint has been the *real* key to defending America's domestic political system and core values. For all of these reasons, Kennan, Lippmann, Morgenthau, Tucker, and Waltz opposed America's Vietnam policy, just as the current generation of realists took the lead in opposing the Iraq war. America's *real* realists have highlighted the dangers that await if the United States gives in to the temptations of primacy and empire and have counseled instead that the United States pursue a grand strategy based on prudence and self-restraint. There are two mechanisms that can constrain the United States. First is a roughly equal distribution of power in the international system, because if confronted by countervailing power the United States would be forced to forego primacy in favor of a more cautious strategy.[38] The other possible restraining mechanism is that America's own domestic political system will prevent "national leaders from dangerous and unnecessary adventures."[39] For the present, at least, there is no counterbalancing power that can compel the United States to forsake its pursuit of primacy and empire. Thus, the United States must follow a policy of self-restraint if it is to avoid primacy's adverse geopolitical and domestic consequences. Since World War II, such self-restraint seldom has been abundant—and has completely vanished during the Bush II administration. Grand strategic self-restraint can be developed only—if at all—by engaging in a vigorous intellectual debate about the consequences of primacy and empire and about America's grand strategic options—and only if that debate carries over into the public policy arena.[40] Here, the torch has been passed to a new generation of realists both to make the case against American Empire and its accompanying perils and to simultaneously make the case for a new U.S. grand strategy.

Notes

1. The classic studies are Robert Gilpin, *War and Change in World Politics* (Cambridge, UK: Cambridge University Press, 1981); Paul Kennedy, *The Rise and Fall of the Great Powers: Economic Change and Military Conflict from 1500 to 2000*) New York: Random House, 1987).

2. Thus, as Edward Luttwak has observed, for both the Roman Empire and the United States, "the elusive goal of strategic statecraft was to provide security for the civilization without prejudicing the vitality of its economic base and without compromising the stability of an evolving political order." Edward Luttwak, *The Grand Strategy of the Roman Empire: From the First Century A.D. to the Third* (Cambridge, Mass.: Harvard University Press, 1976), p. 1.

3. Robert Gilpin, *The Political Economy of International Relations* (Princeton, N.J.: Princeton University Press, 1987), p. 332.

4. In March 2006, GM announced that it would buy out the contracts of all 113,000 unionized employees in its workforce and the contracts of the 13,000 unionized workers at its main parts supplier, Delphi. Micheline Maynard, "GM Will Offer Buyouts to All Its Union Workers," *New York Times*, March 23, 2006, p. A1.

5. Peter G. Gosselin, "That Good Education Might Not Be Enough," *Los Angeles Times*, 6 March 2006, http://www.nytimes.com/2006/03/23/business/23auto.html?ex=1300770000&en=57ea081b0a798618&ei=5088&par.

6. Editorial, "Tackling America's Growing Inequality," *Financial Times*, April 6, 2006, http://news.ft.com/cms/s/d4cf3508-c509-11da-b7c1-000077932430,s01=1.html.

7. This term is Niall Ferguson's. Niall Ferguson, *Colossus: The Price of America's Empire* (New York: Penguin Press, 2004), p. 262.

8. Ibid. As Ferguson says, "America's fiscal overstretch is far worse today than anything [Kennedy] envisaged sixteen years ago."

9. American budget and trade deficits have not been a serious problem heretofore, because U.S. creditors have believed that the United States could repay its debts. There are signs that this may be changing. If, whether for economic or, conceivably, *geopolitical* reasons, others are no longer willing to finance American indebtedness, Washington's choices will be stark: significant dollar devaluation to increase U.S. exports (which will cause inflation and lower living standards) or raising interest rates sharply to attract foreign capital inflows (which will shrink domestic investment and worsen America's long-term economic problems). Given the de-industrialization of the U.S. economy over the past three decades, it is questionable whether, even with a dramatically depreciated dollar, the United States could export enough to make a major dent in its foreign debt. For discussion, see Gilpin, *The Political Economy of International Relations*, p.332.

10. From the American standpoint, the most frightening soft-balancing scenario is the prospect that—more for geopolitical than economic reasons—the EU, China, and other key players (like OPEC) will collaborate to have the euro supplant the dollar as the international economic system's reserve currency.

11. See Niall Ferguson and Laurence J. Kotlikoff, "Going Critical: American Power and the Consequences of Fiscal Overstretch," *National Interest* 73 (Fall 2003): 22–32. Also, see Laurence J. Kotlikoff and Scott Burns, *The Coming Generational Storm: What You Need to Know about America's Economic Future* (Cambridge, Mass.: MIT Press, 2004).

12. Alternatively, the United States could raise taxes dramatically. This would have negative long-term consequences for the economy, however. More importantly, perhaps, it is not clear that if confronted with a stark choice between hegemony or domestic welfare whether congress or the public would accept being taxed at very high rates in order to sustain American preponderance.

13. See Edmund L. Andrews, "80% of Budget Effectively Off Limits to Cuts," *New York Times*, April 6, 2006, p. A22; Jonathan Weisman, "Years of Deep Cuts Needed to Meet Goal on Deficit, Data Show," *Washington Post*, February 9, 2006, p. A4; Amy Goldstein, "2007 Budget Favors Defense," *Washington Post*, February 5, 2006, p. A1.

14. See Martin Wolff, "America Failed to Calculate the Enormous Costs of War," *Financial Times*, January 11, 2006, p. 15.

15. See Mark Mazetti, "Military at Risk, Congress Warned," *Los Angeles Times*, May 3, 2005, p. A1. http://www.latimes.com/news/printedition/front/la-na-strategy3may03; Thom Shanker, "Pentagon Says Iraq Effort Limits Ability to Fight Other Conflicts," *New York Times*, 3 May 2005, www.nytimes.com/2005/05/03/politics/03military.html?ex=1272772 800&en=2913a0da89d938a3&ei=5090&...; Ann Scott Tyson, "Two Years Later, Iraq War Drains Military," *Washington Post*, 19 March 2005, p. A1. Facing troop shortages, the Defense Department apparently has concluded that it will need allied military support to undertake future military interventions and subsequent occupations. The Terms of Reference for the Pentagon's 2005 Quadrennial Defense Review states that current security challenges "are such that the United States cannot succeed by addressing them alone." Quoted in Thom Shanker, "Pentagon Invites Allies for First Time to Secret Talks Aimed at Sharing Burdens," *New York Times*, March 18, 2005, http://www.nytimes.com/2005/03/18/politics/18strategy.html. Also see Mark Mazetti, "Iraq War Compels Pentagon to Rethink Big-Picture Strategy," *Los Angeles Times*, 11 March 2005, http://www.latimes.com/news/printedition/front/la-na-milwarllmar11. It is doubtful whether allied help will be forthcoming in the future, however. One of the clear lessons of Iraq is that if American allies disagree with U.S. policy, they will withhold military support.

16. Gilpin, *Political Economy of International Relations*, pp. 347–348. For a more recent iteration of this analysis of U.S economic prospects, see Peter G. Peterson, *Running on Empty: How the Democratic and Republican Parties Are Bankrupting Our Future and What Americans Can Do about It* (New York: Farrar, Straus, and Giroux, 2004).

17. James Risen, *State of War: The Secret History of the CIA and the Bush Administration* (New York: Free Press, 2006), pp. 43–44.

18. Ibid., p. 52.

19. Barton Gellman, "The FBI's Secret Scrutiny," *Washington Post*, November 6, 2005, p. A1.

20. Ibid.

21. The Patriot Act's admonition that the existence of national security letters cannot be disclosed is being challenged in the federal courts, notably in the case of *Library Connection, Inc. v. Gonzales*.

22. On U.S. torture policy, see Seymour Hersh, *Chain of Command: The Road from 9/11 to Abu Ghraib* (New York: HarperCollins, 2004); Karen Greenberg, ed., *The Torture Papers: The Road to Abu Ghraib* (Cambridge, UK: Cambridge University Press, 2005). On the CIA's secret overseas prison system, see Dana Priest, "CIA Holds Terror Suspects in Secret Prisons," *Washington Post*, November 2, 2005, p. A1.

23. Stephen M. Walt, *Taming American Power: The Global Response to U.S. Primacy* (New York: W.W. Norton, 2005), p. 232.

24. Ibid.

25. On both torture "lite" and the debate about the effectiveness of torture as a means of extracting reliable intelligence data, see Joseph Lelyveld, "Interrogating Ourselves," *New York Times Sunday Magazine*, June 12, 2005. http://www.nytimes.com/2005/06/12/magazine/12TORTURE. html.

26. Louis Fisher, *Presidential War Power*, 2d ed. Rev. (Lawrence: University Press of Kansas, 2004), pp. 234–235.

27. Seymour Hersh, "The Coming Wars," *The New Yorker*, January 24, 2005., www.newyorker.com/fact/content/?050124fa_fact.

28. Fisher, *Presidential War Power*, pp. 234–235.

29. Kenneth N. Waltz, *Theory of International Politics* (Reading, Mass.: Addison-Wesley, 1979), p. 201.

30. Waltz, "Reply to My Critics," in Robert O. Keohane, ed., *Neorealism and Its Critics* (New York: Columbia University Press, 1986), p. 341.

31. Edmund Burke, *The Works of Edmund Burke* (Boston: Little, Brown, 1901), Vol. IV, p. 457.

32. Walter LaFeber, "The Bush Doctrine," *Diplomatic History* 26 (4): 558.

33. Waltz, *Theory of International Politics*, p. 201.

34. Greg Russell shows that Morgenthau "refused to consider the national interest as a static, self-evident principle of statecraft whose formulation is immune from the complex interaction of domestic and external influences on the decision-making process in foreign policy." Greg Russell, *Hans J. Morgenthau and the Ethics of American Statecraft* (Baton Rouge: Louisiana State University Press, 1990), p. 104.

35. Michael Joseph Smith, *Realist Thought from Weber to Kissinger* (Baton Rouge: Louisiana State University Press, 1987), p. 164.
36. W. David Clinton, *The Two Faces of National Interest* (Baton Rouge: Louisiana State University Press, 1994), p. 259.
37. Frank Ninkovich, *Modernity and Power: A History of the Domino Theory in the Twentieth Century* (Chicago: University of Chicago Press, 1994), p. 53.
38. Waltz, *Theory of International Politics*, p. 206.
39. Ibid.
40. The only viable alternative to the strategy of primacy and empire is an offshore balancing grand strategy. For a detailed discussion of offshore balancing, see Christopher Layne, *The Peace of Illusions: American Grand Strategy from 1940 to the Present* (Ithaca, N.Y.: Cornell University Press, 2006), chap. 8.

Suggested Reading

The American Empire: Overview

Bacevich, Andrew J. *American Empire: The Realities and Consequences of U.S. Diplomacy.* Cambridge, Mass.: Harvard University Press, 2002.

Bacevich, Andrew J. *The New American Militarism: How Americans Are Seduced by War.* New York: Oxford University Press, 2005.

Boot, Max. *The Savage Wars of Peace: Small Wars and the Rise of American Power.* New York: Basic Books, 2002.

Eland, Ivan. *The Empire Has No Clothes: U.S. Foreign Policy Exposed.* Oakland, Calif.: Independent Institute, 2004.

Ferguson, Niall. *Colossus: The Price of America's Empire.* New York: Penguin, 2004.

Johnson, Chalmers. *Blowback: The Costs and Consequences of American Empire.* New York: Metropolitan Books, 2000.

Odom, William E. *America's Inadvertent Empire.* New Haven, Conn.: Yale University Press, 2004.

American Empire: The Historical Context

LaFeber, Walter. *The New Empire: An Interpretation of American Expansion, 1860–1898.* Ithaca, N.Y.: Cornell University Press, 1997.

Van Alstyne, Richard. *The Rising American Empire.* New York: W.W. Norton, 1974.

Williams, William Appleman. *The Tragedy of American Diplomacy.* New York: W.W. Norton, 1988.

Costs and Consequences of American Empire

Hersh, Seymour. *Chain of Command: The Road from 9/11 to Abu Ghraib.* New York: HarperCollins, 2004.

Johnson, Chalmers. *The Sorrows of Empire: Militarism, Secrecy, and the End of the Republic.* New York: Metropolitan Books, 2004.

Phillips, Kevin. *American Theocracy: The Perils and Politics of Radical Religion, Oil and Borrowed Money in the 21st Century.* New York: Viking, 2006.

Risen, James. *State of War: The Secret History of the CIA and the Bush Administration.* New York: Free Press, 2006.

American Hegemony and U.S. Grand Strategy

Art, Robert J. *A Grand Strategy for America.* Ithaca, N.Y.: Cornell University Press, 2003.

Brown, Michael E., et al., eds. *America's Strategic Choices.* Cambridge, Mass.: MIT Press, 2000.

Brzezinski, Zbigniew. *Out of Control: Global Turmoil on the Eve of the Twenty-First Century.* New York: Scribner, 1993.

Brzezinski, Zbigniew. *The Choice: Global Domination or Global Leadership.* New York: Basic Books, 2004.

Brzezinski, Zbigniew. *The Grand Chessboard: American Primacy and Its Geostrategic Imperatives.* New York: Basic Books, 1997.

Buchanan, Patrick J. *A Republic, Not an Empire: Reclaiming America's Destiny.* Washington, D.C.: Regnery, 1999.

Cooper, Robert. *The Breaking of Nations: Order and Chaos in the Twenty-First Century.* New York: Atlantic Monthly Press, 2003.

Daalder, Ivo H., and James M. Lindsay. *America Unbound: The Bush Revolution in Foreign Policy.* Washington, D.C.: Brookings Institution, 2003.

Gaddis, John Lewis. *Surprise, Security, and the American Experience.* Cambridge, Mass.: Harvard University Press, 2004.

Gray, Colin S. *Modern Strategy*. New York: Oxford University Press, 1999.

Gray, Colin S. *The Sheriff: America's Defense of the New World Order*. Lexington: University Press of Kentucky, 2004.

Hentz, James J. *The Obligations of Empire: United States' Grand Strategy for a New Century*. Lexington: University Press of Kentucky, 2004.

Huntington, Samuel P. *Who Are We? The Challenges to America's National Identity*. New York: Simon and Schuster, 2004.

Ikenberry, G. John, ed. *America Unrivaled: The Future of the Balance of Power*. Ithaca, N.Y.: Cornell University Press, 2002.

Johnson, Chalmers A. *Blowback: The Costs and Consequences of American Empire*. New York: Metropolitan Books, 2000.

Johnson, Chalmers A. *The Sorrow of Empire: Militarism, Secrecy, and the End of the Republic*. New York: Metropolitan Books, 2004.

Layne, Christopher. *The Peace of Illusions: American Grand Strategy from 1940 to the Present*. Ithaca, N.Y.: Cornell University Press, 2006.

Leffler, Melvyn P. *A Preponderance of Power: National Security, the Truman Administration, and the Cold War*. Stanford , Calif.: Stanford University Press, 1992.

Mandelbaum, Michael. *The Case for Goliath: How America Acts as the World's Government in the Twenty-First Century*. New York: Public Affairs, 2005.

Mead, Walter Russell. *Power, Terror, Peace, and War: America's Grand Strategy in a World at Risk*. New York: Knopf, 2004.

Murray, Williamson. MacGregor Knox, and Alvin Bernstein, eds. *The Making of Strategy: Rulers, States, and War*. New York: Cambridge University Press, 1994.

Nye, Joseph S., Jr. *Governance in a Globalizing World*. Washington, D.C., Brookings Institution Press, 2000.

Nye, Joseph S., Jr. *Soft Power: The Means to Success in World Politics*. New York: Public Affairs, 2004.

Nye, Joseph S., Jr. *The Paradox of American Power: Why the World's Only Superpower Can't Go It Alone*. New York: Oxford University Press, 2002.

Odom, William E., and Robert Dujarric. *America's Inadvertent Empire*. New Haven, Conn.: Yale University Press, 2004.

Walt, Stephen M. *Taming American Power: The Global Response to U.S. Primacy*. New York: W.W. Norton, 2005.

The Bush Administration and U.S. Foreign Policy

Daalder, Ivo H., and James M. Lindsey. *America Unbound: The Bush Revolution in Foreign Policy*. Washington, D.C.: Brookings Institution, 2003.

Gaddis, John Lewis. *Surprise, Security and the American Experience*. Cambridge, Mass.: Harvard University Press, 2004.

Mann, Jim. *The Rise of the Vulcans: The History of Bush's War Cabinet*. New York: Viking, 2004.

Woodward, Bob. *Bush at War*. New York: Simon and Schuster, 2002.

The Neoconservatives and American Foreign Policy

Friedman, Murray. *The Neoconservative Revolution: Jewish Intellectuals and the Shaping of Public Policy*. Cambridge, UK: Cambridge University Press, 2005.

Fukuyama, Francis. *America at the Crossroads: Democracy, Power, and the Neo-Conservative Legacy*. New Haven, Conn.: Yale University Press, 2006.

Halper, Stefan, and Jonathan Clarke. *America Alone: The Neo-Conservatives and the Global Order*. Cambridge, UK: Cambridge University Press, 2004.

China

Carpenter, Ted Galen. *America's Coming War with China: A Collision Course with Japan*. New York: Palgrave Macmillan, 2006.

Goldstein, Avery. *Rising to the Challenge: China's Grand Strategy and International Security*. Stanford, Calif.: Stanford University Press, 2005.

Shambaugh, David, ed. *Power Shift: China's and Asia's New Dynamics*. Berkeley: University of California Press, 2006.

Tucker, Nancy Bernkopf. *Dangerous Strait: The U.S.–Taiwan–China Crisis*. New York: Columbia University Press, 2005.

Iraq

Danner, Mark. *The Secret Way to War: The Downing Street Memo and the Iraq War's Buried History*. New York: New York Review of Books, 2006.

Diamond, Larry. *Squandered Victory: The American Occupation and the Bungled Effort to Bring Democracy to Iraq*. New York: Times Books, 2004.

Gordon, Michael R., and Bernard E. Trainor. *Cobra II: The Inside Story of the Invasion and Occupation of Iraq*. New York: Pantheon, 2006.

Hashim, Ahmed S. *Insurgency and Counter-Insurgency in Iraq*. Ithaca, N.Y.: Cornell University Press, 2006.

Packer, George. *The Assassin's Gate*. New York: Farrar, Strauss, and Giroux, 2005.

Pollack, Kenneth M. *The Threatening Storm: The Case for Invading Iraq*. New York: Random House, 2002.

Rosen, Gary, ed. *The Right War? The Conservative Debate on Iraq*. Cambridge, UK: Cambridge University Press, 2005.

Woodward, Bob. *Plan of Attack*. New York: Simon & Schuster, 2004.

Iran

Berman, Ilan. *Tehran Rising: Iran's Challenge to the United States*. Lanham, Md.: Rowman and Littlefield, 2005.

Keddie, Nikki R. *Modern Iran: Roots and Results of Revolution*. New Haven, Conn.: Yale University Press, 2003.

Kinzer, Stephen. *All the Shah's Men: An American Coup and the Roots of Middle East Terror*. Hoboken, N.J.: John Wiley & Sons, 2003.

Pollack, Kenneth M. *The Persian Puzzle: The Conflict between Iran and America*. New York: Random House, 2004.

Sciolino, Elaine. *Persian Mirrors: The Elusive Face of Iran*. New York: Free Press, 2001.

Liberal Ideology, Democracy Promotion, and Regime Change

Brown, Michael E., Sean M. Lynn-Jones, and Steven E. Miller. *Debating the Democratic Peace*. Cambridge, Mass: MIT Press, 1996.

Hartz, Louis. *The Liberal Tradition in America*. New York: Harcourt, 1991.

Hunt, Michael H. *Ideology and U.S. Foreign Policy*. New Haven, Conn.: Yale University Press, 1987.

Kinzer, Stephen. *America's Century of Regime Change from Hawaii to Iraq*. New York: Times Books, 2006.

Lieven, Anatol. *America Right or Wrong: An Anatomy of American Nationalism*. New York: Oxford University Press, 2004.

Mansfield, Edward D., and Jack Snyder. *Electing to Fight: Why Emerging Democracies Go to War*. Cambridge, Mass.: MIT Press, 2005.

Mead, Walter Russell. *Special Providence: American Foreign Policy and How It Changed the World*. New York: Routledge, 2002.

Owen, John M. *Liberal Peace, Liberal War: American Politics and International Security*. Ithaca, N.Y.: Cornell University Press, 2000.

Zakaria, Fareed. *The Future of Freedom: Illiberal Democracy at Home and Abroad*. New York: W.W. Norton, 2003.

Terrorism

Benjamin, Daniel, and Steven Simon. *The Age of Sacred Terror: Radical Islam's War against America*. New York: Random House, 2002.

Benjamin, Daniel, and Steven Simon. *The Next Attack: The Failure of the War on Terror and a Strategy for Getting It Right*. New York: Times Books, 2005.

Byman, Daniel. *Deadly Connections: States that Sponsor Terrorism*. Cambridge, UK: Cambridge University Press, 2005.

Clarke, Richard A. *Against All Enemies: Inside America's War on Terror*. New York: Free Press, 2004.

Hoffman, Bruce. *Inside Terrorism*. New York: Columbia University Press, 1998.
Pape, Robert A. *Dying to Win: The Strategic Logic of Suicide Terrorism*. New York: Random House, 2005.
Scheuer, Michael. *Imperial Hubris: Why the West Is Losing the War on Terror*. Washington, D.C.: Brassey's, 2004.

Index